What Others Are Saying About

Holiness Without the Halo

In their typical simple yet profound, down-to-earth yet up-wardly focused writing, the Briscoes have brought the issue of holiness into clear view. Stuart and Jill break down our misconceptions and build a brilliant and compelling view of authentic holiness as they chart a course for us to embrace it in every aspect of living. Ignore this book to your own peril—the gravity of our fallenness needs the rescue of a book like this!

Joseph M. Stowell
President, Cornerstone University
Grand Rapids, Michigan

With their own clear and practical biblical approach, Stuart and Jill Briscoe untangle the misunderstandings and mistakes that keep many Christians from enjoying the happiness of holiness. Read and apply this book to your life and "the truth shall set you free" (John 8:32).

Warren W. Wiersbe
International Bible Teacher and Author
Lincoln, Nebraska

For many Christians, holiness is challenging to understand and difficult to apply in everyday life. Stuart and Jill Briscoe have translated this crucial doctrine from the ethereal domain of theology classrooms to provide practical instruction and everyday application. Prayers, personal insights and provoking questions add an interactive dimension to this significant work. I highly recommend this book for everyone seeking to know and walk with Jesus and grow in His character.

Gary Benedict
President, The Christian and Missionary Alliance, U.S.
Colorado Springs, Colorado

With their characteristic honesty and humor the Briscoes chase any notion of haughtiness right out of holiness! Stuart and Jill show us how to humbly honor the Holy One, and in the process they surprise us with the realization that holiness is both a happy and healthy pursuit. Read it for yourself, study it as a class, talk about it with a group—your heart will begin to hunger for the Holy One and for the holiness of life that befits those who live in His presence.

John Kitchen
Senior Pastor, Stow Alliance Fellowship
Stow, Ohio

*H*oliness

without the

HALO

Finding Unexpected Joy and Freedom in Holy Living

Stuart & Jill Briscoe

PUBLICATIONS

Holiness without the Halo

Copyright 1993, 2011 Stuart and Jill Briscoe
All rights reserved. Published 2012

ISBN 13: 978-1-936143-17-7
ISBN 10: 1-936143-17-8
ISBN (e-book): 978-1-61958-004-6

Published by CLC Publications

U.S.A.
P.O. Box 1449, Fort Washington, PA 19034

GREAT BRITAIN
51 The Dean, Alresford, Hants SO24 9BJ

AUSTRALIA
P.O. Box 469, Kippa-Ring QLD 4021

NEW ZEALAND
118 King Street, Palmerston North 4410

Printed in the United States of America
First printing March, 2012

This is a revised version of the book originally published under the title
Life, Liberty, and the Pursuit of Holiness.

Contents

FOREWORD

Holiness without the Halo confronts our generation with the reality that everything in life is incomplete. Humankind seems to have the ability with cell phones, worldwide internet connections, and an endless selection of vacation adventures and sporting events to stimulate our every fantasy, but still it all seems to be left wanting. The wanting we feel inside is a desire for completeness, perfection and holiness. It's our desire for the holy (complete and perfect) God who designed us to be holy like Him, but we are not.

Stuart and Jill Briscoe focus on this deepest of all drives in the human soul and urge us to seek for fulfillment in the only place it can be found—a deep relationship with the holy God through Jesus Christ our Lord.

All other attempts we make to find life's sweet spot or to experience the happiness of a complete life fall short, for we trust in things or people who are themselves incomplete and imperfect. Only trusting in the perfect One, the completed One, the Holy One, can give us what our soul longs for. *Holiness without the Halo* is a very practical resource for you to find real holiness.

Marty Berglund
Senior Pastor, Fellowship Alliance Chapel
Medford, New Jersey

INTRODUCTION

I grew up in a small town in the north of England. My father owned a grocery store and was the "leading brother" of a small, very small, Brethren assembly. To my youthful ears the dominant theme of the assembly seemed to be "Come out from them and be separate." This meant that we didn't go to movies (we called them "the pictures") or for many years own a radio (we called it "the wireless") or go to football matches. It also meant that we had no time for the Anglican church, very little for the Methodist church and a "hands off" attitude to the Baptist church. Being separated meant being isolated.

We met in a slightly disreputable building made of corrugated iron and called by the locals "The Tin Chapel," and we were regarded as oddities in our small community. So I grew up embarrassed about my spiritual affiliations and negative about being "separated." I knew that it had something to do with "holiness," but I wasn't sure exactly what, and I came to the conclusion that "holiness" and "separation" were necessary—but preferably in old age. If you had asked me to rate "being holy," "being happy" and "being healthy," I probably would have chosen them in the following order of preference: first, being happy; second, being healthy; third, being holy—on the understanding that when I was no longer young enough to be either happy or healthy I would gladly settle for being holy.

Each year my parents took me to the Keswick Convention on Wednesday afternoon, that being "the half day closing" of our store. This famous convention was much more exciting than the assembly in The Tin Chapel. There were crowds of people, many in exotic dress from distant lands; there were Anglicans, Methodists and Baptists, and the banner over the platform said, "All One in Christ Jesus." I liked that and wondered sometimes why we weren't "all one" back home.

But there was a large fly in the ointment—the convention met for the specific purpose of promoting "practical scriptural holiness." Granted, it wasn't the exact kind promoted in my home church. Some of the speakers were obviously not from the assemblies; they wore the clerical "dog collars" and were called "reverend." They didn't seem to know what I had been told for years—that the only person called "reverend" in the Bible was God! They obviously listened to the radio; and to my intense delight, one of them, Alan Redpath, far from condemning the "worldliness" of professional sports, told a story (in a sermon!) about almost making England's Rugby team. I saw that holiness came in a variety of packages, but that only added confusion to my distaste.

I detected a similar degree of confusion and distaste on the subject of holiness many years later in the congregation I had been called to pastor. So I decided to prepare a series of messages entitled "Life, Liberty and the Pursuit of Holiness." This very clever title (I thought!) was, I should perhaps explain for the benefit of non-American readers, a slight but significant alteration of the famous statement in the Declaration of Independence which states that God has granted human beings certain "inalienable rights," namely "life, liberty and the pursuit of happiness." The insertion of "holiness" for "happiness" was, of course, intentional.

I also knew that "happiness" for many moderns is closely related to a view of "healthiness" (we call it "wellness") which seems to mean a state of holistic well-being covering the emotional, relational and physical waterfront. I suspected that if my congregation had the chance to rate happy, healthy and holy, their preferences would not stray far from those of my youth.

Just as I was beginning my studies on holiness, I saw a TV interview (yes, we had graduated to TV and a radio!) in which President and Mrs. George F.W. Bush were answering questions about church attendance. He was commendably forthright on the subject, but was careful to insist that he and Barbara did not want to come across as "holier than thou."

Presumably this was a politically correct statement made for fear of offending some voters, but it also betrayed an uneasiness common to many. To be in any way involved in "holiness" seems to portray a judgmental attitude in a society which prides itself in "non-judgmental" attitudes, a self-righteousness in a culture which is much more committed to "feeling good" and "looking good" than "being good" and "doing good." In fact, to be called a "do-gooder" is almost as damning as to be accused of being "holier than thou." How strangely inverted is our culture!

In light of the widespread disinterest in holiness in the church and the deep distrust outside the church, it is not surprising that the subject is often treated with benign neglect by the church. In fact, in congregations which emphasize evangelism, the idea of concentrating on being holy may be seen as a luxury they cannot afford, when there are "so many lost people to be won to the Lord."

To those who think this way, I would point out that Dr. Michael Green, the articulate pastor/teacher whose evangelistic zeal and effectiveness are legendary, stated bluntly in his book, *Evangelism Through the Local Church*, "People did not feel that [Christ] was talking down to them or manifesting superiority. They were drawn by His naturalness, His integrity, His unshakableness, His friendliness, His holiness. For true holiness is the greatest magnet of all."[1]

In churches committed to meeting people's needs, the words of Robert Murray McCheyne may come as a surprise: "The greatest need of my people is that I live a holy life." The apostle Peter put it all in current perspective when he encouraged the early Christians, "Just as He who called you is holy, so be holy in all you do. . . . live your lives as strangers here in reverent fear. . . . Live such good lives among the pagans that . . . they may see your good deeds and glorify God" (1 Pet. 1:15, 17; 2:12).

There is no incompatibility between evangelism, discipleship, worship, church life and personal holiness. They are bound up together in a bundle of God's making. Neither is there a conflict between being thoroughly happy, truly healthy and practically holy. Fullness and wholeness of life are found exclusively in relationship to the One who is life, the One who stated unequivocally, "Be holy, because I am holy" (1 Pet. 1:16). By this He obviously did not mean, "Be splendidly isolated, because I exist in splendid isolation." Neither was He suggesting, "Be removed from and disinterested in My wonderful creation, because I am removed from and disinterested in My wonderful creative masterpiece."

What He did mean, and how it applied practically to involved, relevant, positive and powerful living, became the subject of my preaching and, to my great delight, the focus of the congregation's attention, interest and desire.

Jill and I trust that this book will convey the same message to you in an encouraging and helpful manner, and that you will determine, as we and many in our congregation eventually did, to rate "being holy" first with "being happy" and "being healthy" in a dead heat immediately behind, and dependent upon, the front-runner.

1

KNOWLEDGE OF THE HOLY ONE

*The fear of the LORD is the beginning of wisdom, and
knowledge of the Holy One is understanding.* (PROV. 9:10)

Vince Lombardi, the legendary coach of the Green Bay Pack-
ers, was not pleased. In his opinion his team was playing
well below its capability. So he called a special team meeting,
held up a ball and with heavy irony and unveiled sarcasm said
to the professional footballers, "Gentlemen, this is a football!"

One of his more intrepid players held up his hand and asked,
"Could you go over that again, Coach?"

This remark was no doubt dealt with as Lombardi continued making the point, all too obviously, that they were going
to start learning the game again at the very beginning. He was
reintroducing them to fundamentals. In our increasingly complex world, an occasional revisit of fundamentals is usually of
great value!

Speaking of fundamentals, the book of Proverbs says that
"the fear of the LORD is the beginning of wisdom." For "be-

ginning" read "fundamental basis." So the fear of the Lord is to wisdom what a football is to football! Wisdom, one of the dominant themes of the Old Testament, means a lot more than acquiring information or establishing a database. For instance, wisdom is clearly related to "the beginning of knowledge," "discipline," "insight," "prudence," "what is right, just, and fair," "direction" and "guidance" in the introductory verses of Proverbs (Prov. 1:1–7). When taken together, these words describe what we call, in modern terms, "a system of values." So you could say that the fear of the Lord is the fundamental basis of a system of values.

The Fear of the Lord

But what is meant by "the fear of the LORD"? (Notice that the Bible sometimes reads "LORD" and other times "Lord." This is not a printer's error, but a means of distinguishing two different Hebrew words in English.) In Proverbs 9:10 "LORD" is in uppercase letters to designate the name Yahweh or Jehovah—the name by which Israel's God chose to reveal or describe Himself.

This name is shrouded in mystery, but is probably related to the verb "to be." So when Moses, startled by God's commission to go and confront the formidable Pharaoh, asked God about His name, he received the enigmatic reply, "I AM WHO I AM. This is what you are to say to the Israelites: 'I AM has sent me to you'" (Exod. 3:14). So if "I AM WHO I AM" and "Jehovah" are related names and both are linked to the verb "to be," they speak of His *being*-ness, His *am*-ness, His *is*-ness—the uniqueness of His existence!

I am writing this chapter on board the Operation Mobilization ship *Logos Hope*, tied up in the port of Doha, Qatar. Tomorrow we are due to sail for Dubai in the U.A.E., and the following day we set sail for Sri Lanka. So when I explain to people what I am doing, I tell them, "Last week I was in the U.S.A., this week I am in the Gulf and next week, God willing, I will be in Sri Lanka." To which they reply, "Better you than me!" I am thoroughly human and therefore limited by time and space, so I have to talk in tenses and locations: "I was in the U.S.A., I am in the Gulf and I will be in Sri Lanka."

But the LORD, the "I AM WHO I AM," being eternal and omnipresent, has no such limitations. He transcends time and space; He is without beginning or end. He is in U.S.A. and the Gulf and Sri Lanka, all at the same time—and He *always* is there! He needs nothing. He is self-existent and self-sufficient, and as such, He is totally awe-inspiring. To understand this is to respect, to reverence, to fear the LORD.

To many people there is something frightening about fearing the Lord. This is understandable, and we must be careful how we deal with the issue. In my pastoral ministry I find many people whose lives have been so conditioned by "a religion of fear" that they have little or no concept of the joy of salvation and the wonders of amazing grace. But I also meet many people who have been encouraged to concentrate on the love of God and His kindness until they have settled comfortably into what the late German theologian and martyr Dietrich Bonhoeffer called "cheap grace." Their lives all too often demonstrate the old adage: "That which is lightly held is easily dropped."

There is a balance. The psalmist struck it when he wrote, "Serve the Lord with fear, and rejoice with trembling" (Ps. 2:11). And Frederick W. Faber had it right when he wrote,

Oh how I fear Thee, living God!
With deepest, tenderest fears,
And worship Thee with trembling hope
And penitential tears.[2]

When we contemplate the Lord in this way and respond with reverence for Him in our hearts, we have found the fundamental basis of a system of values. Our lifestyles will not be built upon ourselves. Neither will they be founded on our cultural norms. They will be predicated on the unchanging, eternal God who has made Himself known to mankind. He is the One from whom we come, through whom we exist and to whom we are accountable. On this sure foundation the true system of values firmly stands.

Knowledge of the Holy One

Hebrew poetry is full of parallelism. This literary device repeats a statement for emphasis, but the repetition is slightly different from the original statement, thus adding color and richness. The text we are considering is a good example, for it contrasts fear and knowledge, Lord and Holy One, wisdom and understanding. When properly focused, these contrasts add clarity of insight to the subject, similar to the way properly focused binoculars give depth of perception and sharpness of vision to a distant image. So we need to meditate on "knowledge of the Holy One" as well as on "fear of the Lord." The prophet Jeremiah reported:

This is what the Lord says:
"Let not the wise man boast of his wisdom
    or the strong man boast of his strength
    or the rich man boast of his riches,

but let him who boasts boast about this:
that he understands and knows me,
that I am the LORD." (Jer. 9:23–24)

It is worth noting that most of the people who are honored as "celebrities" are known for their education (wisdom) or their physical attributes (strength) or their money (riches) rather than their knowledge of God. It has been pointed out that celebrities are simply people who are famous for being well-known. Nevertheless, they are regarded as objects of curiosity and admiration with a little envy and jealousy thrown in. They are hounded and emulated, sought out and listened to. As a result, they become pace-setters and trendmakers, with a willing public trying hard to keep up with their pace and style. Their "values" become the values of society.

Those who know the Holy One, however, are fully aware that the real secret of life is an intimate relationship with (knowledge of) the Holy One, the Lord. Not that they would object to being a little smarter, prettier and wealthier, but these factors do not determine their value system. Knowing the Holy One and fearing the Lord does.

The Holy One

There is some disagreement among scholars concerning the root meaning of the Hebrew word translated "holy." Some say it comes from a verb meaning "to cut," and we will use this concept to help us define the word.

Suppose you are preparing supper. You are late, flustered, and furiously chopping up the ingredients for a salad. The phone rings. You are distracted and cut your finger. Rushing to pick up the phone, you notice that you have cut off a slice of finger.

Peering at you from among the sliced lettuce and tomatoes sits a piece of your finger. It is separate from the rest of you. It is set apart. Distinctively different from the rest of your body, it is now something else—it is wholly *other*.

No doubt you would not meditate on these thoughts for long, preferring rather to seek medical assistance. But momentary meditation would show that if holy is related to "cut," then your separated piece of finger is proclaiming loudly and clearly that *holy* means "separate, set apart, distinct, different, wholly other." If you wish to lapse into a colloquialism, you might be justified in saying holy means "something else!"

The adjective *holy* is applied in a variety of ways in Scripture. At the conclusion of His initial work of Creation, God rested and declared the seventh day "holy" (Genesis 2:3). This did not mean that this day was a constitutionally different day from other days. But it did mean that it was specifically set apart by God for His purposes and, therefore, was distinct from other days — special, something else. In the same way, the ground on which Moses stood on the far side of the desert was constructed of the same rocks and sand that the surrounding land was made of, but it was nevertheless declared by God to be "holy" (Ex. 3:5). This was so precisely because God had chosen to set it apart for the express purpose of allowing Moses to meet with Him there. So it was "holy ground."

When the Lord reveals Himself to us as the Holy One, He is making a statement concerning His Wholly Otherness. His name Yahweh means that He is quite beyond compare. We would say He is in a league of His own. Or as Jehovah Himself inquired, "To whom will you compare Me? Or who is My equal?" (Isa. 40:25).

The Unclean and the Clean

On one occasion two of Aaron's sons, Nadab and Abihu, took matters into their own hands and engaged in activities contrary to the Lord's command and immediately suffered the consequences of their actions. To explain this to the people, Moses said, "This is what the Lord spoke of when He said: 'Among those who approach Me I will show Myself holy; in the sight of all the people I will be honored'" (Lev. 10:3).

The Lord went on to explain that those who were to approach His holiness "must distinguish between the holy and the profane, between the unclean and the clean" (10:10). From the context it can be seen that the Lord was referring to the ritualistic details which were to be observed if His people were going to have dealings with Him, for the ritual was pointing to a profound reality.

As we have seen, a day could be set apart as holy. A collection of rocks and sand constituting a piece of wilderness real estate was designated holy. Even pots and pans could be identified as holy pots and pans. There was nothing intrinsically different about the nature of these mundane entities. But they were declared holy as opposed to common or profane, and clean as opposed to unclean, in order that the people might recognize that there is a moral aspect—a "cleanness"—to that which is holy. To be holy is to be set apart. The holiness of God therefore, among other things, speaks of His being set apart or totally different from all that is unclean or profane.

In this sense it is relatively easy for us to grasp the holiness of God. He is different, set apart from us in His moral purity as opposed to our moral impurity. His holiness is in sharp, striking relief to our profanity, His cleanness to our uncleanness. The fallenness of our humanity means that even in our noblest moments, in our finest hours, we are not totally free from the taint and warp of our moral imperfection. The best of men is a man at best. Our kindness can be stained by pride, our altruism by egoism, our selflessness by self-aggrandizement. But not the Holy One. He is something else. He is distinctly different from us. He is without taint or warp or any such thing. To understand that and to "know" the Holy One is to be ushered into the presence of reality, the domain of true values.

During the last two decades of the twentieth century, the magnificent frescoes on the ceiling of the Sistine Chapel in the Vatican were cleaned and restored. When the grime and pollution were removed from Michelangelo's masterpieces depicting the Lord's creative work, one reporter exclaimed, "God was seen in a way that He had never been seen for many generations!" There was a vividness of color, a freshness, a glory that had hitherto gone unrecognized until the grime was removed. In much the same way, if we have a faulty vision of God and do not see His holiness, we can have a faulty knowledge of Him and a warped system of values.

The Lord Our God Is Holy

If we were asked what characteristics of God we find most appealing and attractive, my guess is that holiness would not appear very high on the list. Love, grace and kindness would undoubtedly be listed quickly. Omniscience, omnipresence and omnipotence would no doubt appear together. Justice and righteousness would perhaps be a little further down the list, and anger and wrath might just find a place. But what about holiness?

There is a sense in which holiness is the prime characteristic of God; it is like a giant descriptive umbrella. It *defines* His other characteristics—His love, grace and kindness are *holy* love, *holy* grace and *holy* kindness. These holy attributes are so far above our understanding of things as to be virtually unlike anything we know.

The "omni" attributes obviously fall into this category. But it is probably most important for us to see that the characteristics we find less appealing are equally holy. His justice is distinct from the justice we have known. His anger, like His love, is utterly holy, totally pure. Unlike human love which can lapse into sentimentalism that spoils, or human anger that can degenerate into bitter recriminations that destroy, His love and anger are pure and holy. Something else! This is described in Psalm 99:

> The LORD reigns,
>   let the nations tremble;
> he sits enthroned between the cherubim,
>   let the earth shake.
> Great is the LORD in Zion;
>   he is exalted over all the nations.
> Let them praise your great and awesome name—
>   he is holy.
>
> The King is mighty, he loves justice—
>   you have established equity;
> in Jacob you have done
>   what is just and right.
> Exalt the LORD our God
>   and worship at his footstool;
>   he is holy.
>
> Moses and Aaron were among his priests,
>   Samuel was among those who called on his name;
> they called on the LORD
>   and he answered them.

He spoke to them from the pillar of cloud;
    they kept his statutes and the decrees he gave them.

O LORD our God,
    you answered them;
you were to Israel a forgiving God,
    though You punished their misdeeds.
Exalt the LORD our God
    and worship at his holy mountain,
for the LORD our God is holy.

After reciting the details of God's character revealed in His activities, the psalmist repeats the refrain, "He is holy," and then concludes, "The Lord our God is holy." It is His holiness that shines through His actions and is descriptive of His character. And it is His holiness which we should proclaim until the day we join in the eternal exulting song:

Great and marvelous are your deeds,
    Lord God Almighty.
Just and true are your ways,
    King of the ages.
Who will not fear you, O Lord,
    and bring glory to Your name?
For you alone are holy. (Rev. 15:3–4)

A few minutes spent considering the aspects of holiness of which the psalmist speaks will be time well spent.

Majestic

"The Lord reigns, let the nations tremble," says the psalmist (Ps. 99:1). But many people would dismiss this as a misguided statement. A suggestion that the Lord is operative in the affairs of the nations is, in their opinion, incredibly naive. To expect the nations to tremble at this thought is regarded as ludicrous by many intelligent people.

Nevertheless, the alternate worldview—that there is no over-arching authority operative in our world, that events succeed events randomly, meaninglessly and accidentally without rhyme or reason—tends to plunge us into unrelieved despair or ostrich-like denial of the unbearable and the unthinkable. Hardly an attractive alternative. At least in faith there is hope!

However, to believe in an active God who reigns in the affairs of men raises great problems. Given the injustice and the inhu-manity, the corruption and the carnage rampant in our world, we might be forgiven for assuming that there is no reigning Lord—or that if He reigns, His rule leaves much to be desired.

But there is one factor that must not be overlooked: His ho-liness. His rule is holy, without taint or warp, and totally "other" from anything we have known apart from Him.

To believe that God was in charge during the Exodus, to ac-cept that He was in control during the Exile, that He would use cruel Egypt and even more cruel Babylon to further His gracious purposes, required a clear eye of faith that saw beyond the messi-ness of man to the holiness of God and the integrity of His eternal plan. But many of God's ancient people managed to do just that.

In more recent times, to understand that His hand was at work in China in events that appeared disastrous took great faith in the uniqueness of His rule. But He graciously allowed us to see the genius of His working in the greatest people movement in church history, something which probably would not have happened in other circumstances.

Even as I write, unheard-of popular uprisings are roiling the authoritative regimes of North Africa and the Middle East; it is far too early to predict what, from a human point of view, will be the outcome. It may strain credulity to the limit to believe that in the trauma and turmoil of international relations there is a guiding hand steering unerringly toward an ultimate eternal kingdom characterized by righteousness. But it is consistent with God's rule and reign, which is quite apart from and utterly superior to anything we have ever seen—or ever will. In other words, He is holy! The Lord reigns!

Awesome

The psalmist continues: "Let them praise your great and awesome name" (99:3). *Awesome* used to mean "that which fills with awe," but in the second half of the twentieth century, it gradually fell into obsolescence. It seemed outdated in a culture jaded by success and indifferent to triumph.

We had lost our ability to be awestruck. Moon landings became routine; images of the planets beamed across mind-boggling distances ceased to boggle. Earth-shattering events like the collapse of the Soviet empire quickly slid into the wastebaskets of the public consciousness. G.K. Chesterton pointed out many years ago, "The world will never starve for want of wonders, but only for want of wonder." What would he say today?

We rarely needed the old word awesome because we didn't allow ourselves the privilege of being awed. But amazingly, the word made a comeback of sorts in the 1990s. It was reincarnated in an inferior form, much like the legendary wicked prince who returned to earth as a flea. It became a slang term for anything generally positive (like the similarly vague term *cool*). Though fading in popular parlance, awesome now refers to anything from a laser show at a rock concert to a big win in the lottery. The word is used by sportscasters to describe someone scoring a goal with athletic flair.

But we should reserve awesome for something that really engenders feelings of awe; something so unique that there's nothing remotely like it anywhere. Something so beyond anything else that it would be like watching a basketball star soar over the opposition to dunk the ball through the ten-foot hoop—and then turning away just in time to see a Hand take the universe and dunk it! *That* would be awesome!

Those who "see" that sort of thing respond to the exhortation, "Let them praise your great and awesome name—he is holy," because they know the One who can, and who one day will, dunk the universe.

Just and Right

The psalmist affirmed, "You have done what is just and right" (99:4). We tend to be a little confused about justice. We are like the lady who insisted to the young photographer that he should "do her justice," and was told she needed mercy!

As we look at our judicial system, we may wonder to ourselves if the practice of law has not overshadowed the administration of justice. There seem to be some people who, released on a legal technicality, proclaim their "belief in the system"; but they choose not to discuss matters as uncomfortable as whether they actually committed the crime they were accused of and what would have constituted appropriate justice. The venerable Lady Justice stands blindfolded, holding sword and scales in order to dispense impartial judgments; but she may have a hole in her blindfold or be peeping round the edges. There is widespread suspicion that justice is one thing for the rich and another for the poor. You could say that there is an uneasy feeling of injustice in the air.

But those who complain about "miscarriages of justice" often desire a "justice" for themselves that gives them a break instead of what they deserve. R.C. Sproul discovered this when he began his teaching career. He told his class to present three papers on time as stipulated, or they would get an F. Many of his students missed the deadline for the first paper, so he relented. A larger number failed to submit the second paper on time and were even blasé about it. He read them the riot act, but gave no Fs.

When the third paper date came and went and even more students missed the deadline, he kept his promise and gave them an F. They were furious that he would do such a thing! One student demanded that he reverse his decision because it was so unfair. Dr. Sproul asked the young man if he really wanted to be treated fairly, and he replied in the affirmative. "All right, you didn't get any papers in on time, so you get three Fs." There was an uproar, but there was also justice—impartial, consistent and unpopular!

Ideas about justice have become desperately confused. But there is a reference point. The Lord can be counted on to do what is "just and right," for He is holy. This means, of course, that His blindfold has not slipped because He wears none. He needs none. His justice and righteousness are pure and right—utterly and intrinsically. He is something else!

They Called and He Answered

One of the dangers of concentrating on the awesome, majestic righteousness of God is that He becomes so overwhelming as to appear unapproachable. We will explore this further in the next chapter, but here I want to say that He hears and answers the pleas and prayers of His people. His holiness does not negate His availability or His accessibility.

Moses and Aaron were among His priests,
> Samuel was among those who called on His name;
they called on the LORD
> and he answered them.
He spoke to them from the pillar of cloud;
> they kept His statutes and the decrees he gave them.

O LORD our God,
> you answered them;
you were to Israel a forgiving God,
> though You punished their misdeeds.
Exalt the LORD our God
> and worship at His holy mountain,
> for the LORD our God is holy. (99:6–9)

Far from being so shrouded in remote holiness that He cannot be approached, the Lord has made known His desire to be known and heard, honored and revered. First, through leaders like Moses and Aaron, He made elaborate provision for His ancient people to recognize His presence in their midst and approach His holiness. Then in Christ He provided "a new and living way" into His presence, and He invites us to "have confidence to enter the most holy place" (Heb. 10:19–20), there to "receive mercy and find grace to help us in our time of need" (4:16).

The awesome holiness of God should hold no terror for the child of God, only reverence and deep humility. It should, however, give pause to those who treat Him and His grace with disrespect. To them it should be made clear that "It is a dreadful thing to fall into the hands of the living God" (10:31).

Yet, because His grace and mercy are holy and pure, it is a wonderful thing to rest in the arms of the forgiving God. He is holy! He is something else!

But you may ask, "What possible connection is there between the holiness of God and the happiness of me? How do I make the leap from His extraordinary otherness to my ordinary happiness?" You examine the fundamental values on which your life rests and your happiness depends, to see whether or not all that you are and have and do and plan are related to who He is and what He wills. If so, a deep-rooted sense of well-being, the essence of happiness, will be yours. But if you have a system of values based on an inferior foundation, you will experience something considerably less than the "joy unspeakable" or "the peace that passes understanding" which are the stuff of real happiness.

PRAYER

Forgive us, dear Lord, for we tend to be desperately self-centered. It is not that we should not be concerned about ourselves; our tragedy is that our self-centeredness so often means we have little sense of who You are; and accordingly, we fail utterly to see ourselves in perspective. When we do meditate upon You, we frequently are very selective in the characteristics that we embrace.

We ask that by Your Spirit You would help us to rightly understand what Your Word is saying and to rightly respond and come humbly before You, claiming no merits of our own. In the light of our sinfulness before Your purity and our creatureliness before Your otherness, we seek only that You will be gracious to us, and for Christ's sake forgive us, and so work in our lives that You will make us distinctly, delightfully, deliciously different—a holy people.

We pray in the name of our Lord Jesus, the Holy One. Amen.

A PERSONAL NOTE FROM JILL

When I was very young, I believed that all wisdom definitely resided in my mother. She alone was the fount of all knowledge, the safest and surest way to find the truth about my small world. As I burst into my turbulent teens, my friends replaced her. Together we rearranged the parental values we agreed had been laid upon us into a more comfortable place to live.

By the time college rolled around, I decided to rationalize my sin and call it growing up. This was after a boyfriend suggested if I had never been drunk, my maturity was suspect and my education somewhat lacking! Such maturity and knowledge went together, he insisted.

Then I became ill and was rushed to the hospital. Here my view of what was really important was redefined in a hurry! Life and health became a sudden and vital necessity. These basic values were modeled by a dedicated medical staff. Up to this point I had put no value on death whatsoever. "Why should youth value age?" I reasoned.

The Scriptures command us, "Remember your Creator in the days of your youth, before the days of trouble come and the years approach when you will say, 'I find no pleasure in them'" (Eccles. 12:1). But I had never read this particular verse—and if I had, would have considered it a very upside-down way of doing things!

Facing this immediate medical crisis focused my eighteen-year-old life. It also taught me that fears revealed my value system. The trivial concerns my protected environment had produced to this point in my life had to do with fears of failure—of my place on the tennis team or losing my boyfriend. Now I realized that what I feared, I valued. Brought face-to-face with death and the possibility of my personal demise, I realized the "light" value I had placed upon life itself, my very existence as a person. Then and only then did I begin to fear the Lord! He, after all, was the One who held my life in His hands.

And so I came to Christ and my focus did an about-face. My family and friends stood back in shock as I began to be involved in church, Bible studies, prayer and witnessing. Now I was discovering that we spend our time doing the things we value most! In other words, our activities give a clue to our value system! This was where wisdom began for me. Now I believed that Jesus was the point of all knowledge, His Word the explanation. He is *the* truth, not *a* truth. And for me, it has been so ever since.

CHAPTER QUESTIONS

Define six basic approaches as to how we arrive at a personal value system. Discuss which approach has been nearest to your own:

- authority
- logic
- sense experience
- emotion
- intuition
- science

If the basis of your value system has been faulty, list the practical steps you can take to put it right.

1. At the very beginning of his reign, Solomon had an incredible dream. Read about it in First Kings 3:5-15. Then discuss:

    a. If God had given you the opportunity to make one wish come true, what would you have asked Him for? Be honest!

    b. Solomon didn't ask for health, and he didn't ask for wealth. What did he ask for? What was God's response?

2. Make a list of all that God gave Solomon (1 Kings 4:29–

34; 3:13; 10:1–29). Does this mean if you ask for the right things, God will make you rich too?

3. Solomon came to his own good conclusions about a system of values that would bring satisfaction. Yet knowing better, he experimented with a variety of experiences to see what would really work. Many of us who also know better try to find a satisfactory philosophy of life this way too. Read Ecclesiastes 2:1–11; list and discuss all the things Solomon tried. What was his conclusion?

4. It was King Solomon who wrote, "The fear of the Lord is the beginning of wisdom, and knowledge of the Holy One is understanding" (Prov. 9:10). Unfortunately, the king didn't always take his own advice or practice what he preached, but the Scriptures tell us in his youth he was the wisest man alive. Though he started well, it's not how a man starts his walk with God that matters, but how he finishes it. What was Solomon's undoing? Discuss.

5. Trace King Solomon's downfall (1 Kings 10:24–11:8):

   a. First step: Silver and gold (10:24–27)
      Why was this wrong? (See Deut. 17:17.)
   b. Second step: Multiplying horses (10:28–29)
      Why was this wrong? (See Deut. 17:16.)
   c. Third step: Wives (11:3)
      Why was this wrong? (See Deut. 17:19.)
   d. Fourth step: Idolatry (20:1–5)
   e. Result (11:9–11)

What can we learn from all of this? Discuss.

Pray about It

Praise   for helpful thoughts;
the attributes of God;
for healthy Christian heritages;
for the church;
for nurturing groups or anything or
    anyone who has helped you understand
    the concepts of this chapter.

Personal   silent response to the lesson.

Petitions   for those in your family or extended family
    who are not basing their value system
    on the right foundation.

2

֍

HOLY, HOLY, HOLY

Holy, holy, holy is the LORD Almighty;
the whole earth is full of his glory. (ISA. 6:3)

The God of Abraham established His people in the land of promise. Through Moses He reminded them of the covenant He had made with Abraham and outlined His expectations. The people of the covenant were expected to act in accordance with His commandments as an expression of their love for Him, the One who had set His love upon them. In keeping with His commitment to doing what is just and right, He laid out for the people the advantages and disadvantages of obedience and disobedience. There was no confusion concerning the consequences—good or bad—that would attend their actions: "If you are willing and obedient, you will eat the best from the land," He explained, "but if you resist and rebel, you will be devoured by the sword" (Isa. 1:19–20).

The history of God's people is full of examples of those who chose to be "willing and obedient" and those who preferred to "resist and rebel." There were times when the people lived in happy, peaceful and fruitful communion with the Lord, and also times of incredible tension, upheaval, violence and bloodshed.

At one point in the history of Israel, political violence had reached a stage beyond belief. A summary of that period, detailed in Second Kings 15, looked like this:

- Zechariah the son of Jeroboam reigned six months and then was assassinated.
- His assassin, Shallum, reigned one month before he too was assassinated.
- His assassin, Menahem, reigned ten years and remarkably died naturally.
- His son Pekahiah reigned two years but then was assassinated.
- His assassin, Pekah, reigned twenty years before he too was assassinated.

While a lot of the bloodletting was going on in Israel, King Uzziah (also known as Azariah) was reigning in Judah; for much of his reign, the people enjoyed, as promised, "the best from the land." One would have thought that living, as they were, in each other's backyards, Israel and Judah would have believed what the Lord had said; they could see the difference between divine favor and divine judgment being lived out in their own neighborhoods. But it was not to be.

King Uzziah came to the throne at the age of sixteen. In his early days He was instructed "in the fear of God" by Zechariah the priest and was privileged to be ministered to by the gifted prophet Isaiah as his reign progressed. But eventually even he succumbed to disobedience and lived out the balance of his life a shadow of his former self.

There can be no doubt that his demise deeply hurt Isaiah; and this, coupled with the tragic events in neighboring Israel, caused Isaiah to lament, "Ah, sinful nation, a people loaded with guilt, a brood of evildoers, children given to corruption! They have forsaken the Lord; they have spurned the Holy One of Israel and turned their backs on Him" (Isa. 1:4).

If knowledge of the Holy One is wisdom, then spurning the Holy One spells disaster. Isaiah knew it, but felt powerless to stem the tide of rebellion. Then something very dramatic happened in the year that King Uzziah died.

A Vision of the Holy, Holy, Holy God

We are not told the circumstances. All we know is that Isaiah was granted a vision of God. Even Moses was denied his request to see God's glory and was permitted only the most glancing of glimpses. Men in the mortal state do not see God and live to tell their story, unless He comes to them incarnate. So we do not know how exactly Isaiah saw what he saw, but he recorded for posterity what he saw and what he heard.

He saw a "throne high and exalted" and a robe the train of which seemed to fill the temple. When Diana married Charles, Prince of Wales, in St. Paul's Cathedral, the BBC cameramen captured many memorable images. The one that stands out in my mind is the panoramic view, from high in the cathedral's dome, showing the length of Diana's train, which appeared to stretch for many yards behind her as she made her way to her waiting Prince and the Archbishop. A small train would not have matched such a splendid occasion. Her train did not exactly fill

the temple or even the cathedral, but its sheer size spoke power-
fully to the significance of the event.

Isaiah's posture, we suspect, was not such that he had a panoramic view. He was in all probability prostrate before the throne
just inside the temple threshold, which subsequently shook and
shuddered beneath him. As he dared to lift his eyes, he saw only
the vast train of the robe filling his vision and dominating the
scene. High and exalted was the One to whom the train belonged; Isaiah gave no description of the Lord, saying only, "I
saw the Lord." Apparently it was His awesome majesty which
impressed itself on the prophet's consciousness—a marked contrast to the almost total disregard of the Lord on the part of the
people to whom the prophet spoke.

Six-Winged Seraphim

Isaiah's vision and description of the angelic attendants called
seraphim is slightly more detailed. They each had six wings. But
it was what they were calling out to each other that grabbed his
attention: "Holy, holy, holy is the LORD Almighty; the whole
earth is full of His glory" (Isa. 6:3).

The temple was shaken and filled with smoke as a result of
their proclamation. It was not the voice of God which made the
temple rock and caused His majesty and glory to be veiled in
smoke. It was the force and power of the attendants' *testimony
to His holiness*!

The triple repetition "Holy, holy, holy!" conveyed the most
intense expression of holiness. Perhaps to say "Holy, holier, ho-
liest!" would achieve a similar result. At any rate, there was no
doubt in Isaiah's mind about the subject of their worship and
testimony: it was the holiness of the Lord Almighty—*Jehovah
Sabaoth*. This name is descriptive of the One Isaiah saw. Liter-

ally translated, it means "Lord of Hosts" or "Lord of Mighty Armies."

In the heyday of the late Soviet Union, May Day was the annual occasion for pomp and circumstance. May Day was the heyday, you might say! On that day a group of squat, somber, muffled men would file stiffly on to the top of Lenin's mausoleum and the parade would begin. Thousands upon thousands of goose-stepping troops, along with tanks, missiles and personnel carriers, would file past as jets roared overhead.

To the bureaucrats this was a deeply satisfying display of their power—they were the lords of mighty armies! To the watching populace it was intended to be greatly encouraging. They had little cheer in their drab lives, but they could cheer the troops, their powerful defenders, and take heart. And the watching world could tremble appropriately and wonder how to combat such awesome might.

The seraphim of the Lord of armies were His only "troops" on parade that day. He has vast hosts at His disposal, but the seraphim were all that were needed to convey the message to Isaiah. The Holy, Holy, Holy One was awesome in power and ability. Isaiah got the message.

See His six-winged seraphim flying to do His will! Two wings showed their alacrity (flying), and two their humility (covered faces), and the other two their servility (covered feet) as they demonstrated their instant obedience, their glad service, their joyful availability. By such a vast, obedient, joyful host is Lord Sabaoth honored and worshiped. He is holy—*utterly other*!

Centuries after Isaiah, the converted Rabbi Paul pondered the awesome power of the Lord, and in a moment of praise and benediction, he wrote to the Ephesian believers, "Now unto Him who is able to do immeasurably more than all we ask or imagine, according to His power that is at work within us, to Him be glory in the church and in Christ Jesus throughout all generations, forever and ever! Amen" (Eph. 3:20–21).

The Whole Earth

The seraphim proclaimed, "The whole earth is full of the Lord's glory." If Isaiah had not been so overwhelmed by his experience, he might have wondered about that statement. There were many things going on in his world which were less than glorious. The rebellion and resentment on every hand were plain to see. There were and still are many questions that arise in the minds of those who hear of the earth declaring the glory of God and yet see the world displaying the power of evil.

Some see evil triumph and ask why bad things happen to good people. Others, conscious of human sinfulness and concentrating on divine righteousness, wonder why so many good things happen to bad people. To close one's eyes to evil and simply sing God's praises clearly does not address the issue. Yet to be absorbed by evil and lose sight of the wonder of God's handiwork is to sink into a black hole while scanning the universe through the wrong end of the telescope. To insist, "If God is good He is not great; if God is great He is not good," is to assume He must be one or the other, and to deny the biblical revelation of His greatness and goodness.

But the seraphim's statement leaves us with the question, how can a great and good God permit evil? The only satisfactory answer is that God has not stayed aloof from our pain, but has partaken of it at a deeper and more grotesque level than we can ever know. In so doing, He has turned evil on its head, put the devil on his back, and shown conclusively that He who can make even man's wrath praise Him can bring blessing out of buffeting and triumph from the tomb. The cross was the place where God's glory was made known, and from it has flowed down the centuries a glorious stream of blessing into nation after nation. Paul's Ephesian doxology is being fulfilled. God's glory is being seen "in the church and in Christ Jesus throughout all generations." Wherever the church is planted, that part of the earth is full of His glory.

Yet even apart from the church there has always been much of God's glory to be seen. The seraphim were reminding Isaiah of the challenges the Lord Himself has always put before His people. "Do you not know? Have you not heard? The LORD is the everlasting God, the Creator of the ends of the earth" (Isa. 40:28). In the vast and wonderful universe, there is clear evidence of a Creator who pointedly asks mankind, "Lift your eyes and look to the heavens: Who created all these?" (40:26).

The apostle Paul is very specific, insisting that "what may be known about God is plain . . . because God has made it plain. . . . For since the creation of the world God's invisible qualities—His eternal power and divine nature—have been clearly seen, being understood from what has been made" (Rom. 1:19–20). It must be conceded, of course, that the arguments of Hume and Kant and others have placed intellectual roadblocks on the route of trying to reason from an orderly universe to a God of order. As a result, many modern people have found themselves impaled on intimidating philosophical barriers and have failed to recognize how full the earth is of God's glory.

It is not our intention to exhume Hume or to make Kant recant, but simply to say that these men may have shot holes in arguments that were in the first place less than watertight, only to have their own arguments subjected to an intellectual barrage which has left them less than intact. And after the philosophical dust has settled, no doubt to be stirred again, the fact remains that the biblical truth stands firm, towering over the wrecks of arguments, and still pointing us unerringly to a world that says something profound about a God knowable only through revelation—of which creation is a part.

The glory of God is seen in "the whole earth" not only because He created it, but also because He continues to be active in His creation. Diogenes Allen, in his book *Christian Belief in a Post-Modern World*, says, "According to the Christian doctrine of creation, the creation of the universe is not an event in the past that is over and done with, so that once the universe is created, it runs on its own without the need for any divine activity. God's creative activity is continuous."[3]

Scientists have shown that two parts of the gas called hydrogen carefully related to one part of the gas called oxygen regularly produces a liquid called water. This "proves" that $H_2 + O = H_2O$, that the one causes the other. For most people this is sufficient knowledge and an adequate explanation. Science says it all!

But it is equally true to say that God creates water, because for hydrogen and oxygen and water "to exist and to be causally related, God's creative agency must be operating."[4] This being so, we realize that we live in an incredibly complex and wonderful world operating on laws which are discernible and recognizable, which in themselves are the product of God's ongoing creative activity. Even the rain splashing on my window is a thing of wonder—a cause for worship!

Elizabeth Barrett Browning captured something of the wonder of God's creative genius and the pathos of failure to recognize it:

Earth's crammed with heaven,
And every common bush afire with God;
But only he who sees, takes off his shoes,
The rest sit round it and pluck blackberries.[5]

The seraphim and Isaiah were not plucking blackberries. They were tuned in to the fact that the whole earth is full of the glory of the thrice-holy God.

Adonai

We have already seen that LORD = Jehovah. Now we need to note that Lord = Adonai. It was Adonai, the One in whom authority resides, whom Isaiah saw seated on a throne.

His holiness and uniqueness are seen not only in His power and ability as "Lord Sabaoth" or even in His glory demonstrated in the whole earth. His holy, unique authority needs to be recognized too, in order that mankind might rightly relate to Him.

Isaiah's great book starts out with the Holy One of Israel objecting to the desperate behavior of His people. He makes no apology for His complaint; in His capacity as the ultimate authority figure, He determines correct action and evaluates behavior accordingly:

Hear, O heavens! Listen, O earth!
    For the LORD has spoken:
"I reared children and brought them up,
    but they have rebelled against me.
The ox knows his master,
    the donkey his owner's manger,
but Israel does not know,
    my people do not understand." (ISA. 1:2–3)

If you remember the emphasis on knowledge and understanding from Proverbs 9:10, you will note the complete ab-
sence of both in these people—they do not know, they do not
understand. The Lord does not complain and leave it at that. He
insists, "Take your evil deeds out of my sight! Stop doing wrong,
learn to do right!" (1:16–17).

Adonai's authority is such that He determines what is right
or wrong. He is the source of absolute standards—something
that contemporary people who insist that "everything is relative"
are reluctant to acknowledge. They apparently fail to notice that
their statement—"everything is relative"—is an absolute and
therefore is self-contradictory.

As we have already seen, Adonai's authority also determines
the consequences of actions. Humans enjoy a great deal of freedom, but there is one freedom they deeply desire which they are
flatly denied. That is the freedom not only to choose a course of
action, but also to determine the consequences of that action.
Adonai is not prepared, however, to surrender His ordained
principle "You reap what you sow." Our society would like no-
fault choices to go along with no-fault insurance and no-fault
divorce. Society may grant this, but heaven will not.

God's freedom to determine consequences is clearly demonstrated in His reaction to Israel's and Judah's rejection of Him
and His ways. He did something that was unthinkable! He actually determined that His people should not only be punished for
their sin, but incredibly (from His people's point of view) He
announced that the punishment would come in the form of an
invasion by hostile pagan hordes.

The people of God were used to assuming a superior attitude
toward the surrounding nations—an attitude they felt was appropriate for those who had received the covenants and on whom

God's favor had come to rest. The average Israelite saw himself as "a guide for the blind, a light for those who are in the dark, an instructor of the foolish, a teacher of infants" (Rom. 2:19-20). This led him to believe that his status would be preserved.

Israelites were convinced that they held an invulnerable position. It would never occur to them that they could be punished by God. Were not God's purposes dependent on them? How could God challenge the nations around them if they themselves were rendered inoperative by divine judgment? No, that would never happen. God was far too smart to cut off His nose to spite His face!

But Isaiah knew better. In fact, he not only recognized the impending judgment, but foresaw that it would come through the other nations: "He lifts up a banner for the distant nations, he whistles for those at the ends of the earth. Here they come, swiftly and speedily" (5:26). They were about to be as shocked by God's action as American Christians would be if the Lord allowed al Qaeda to invade the US and establish a fundamentalist Islamic state from sea to shining sea. Could that ever happen? No way!

That's how they were thinking in Isaiah's day, but they were forgetting that Adonai—the Holy One—was in charge! However much we might maneuver and manipulate, we will not be able to move Adonai from His position as ultimate authority—He who determines what is morally acceptable and decides the consequences of actions. We need to recognize the awesome Adonai, acknowledge divinely ordained limits, and then live joyfully and freely within them, delighting in His guidance, which leads us in "the paths of righteousness." (Ps. 23:3).

The vision of divine holiness which Isaiah was privileged to behold and record for us had a dramatic and timely effect upon him. To this we now turn our attention.

A Vision of Woe

To put it mildly, Isaiah was overwhelmed by what he saw and heard. In the course of his prophetic ministry, he had been called upon to pronounce "woe" to the people. No one who has a heart for people particularly relishes this kind of assignment, and those who are more concerned about being popular than being faithful will avoid the responsibility.

But Isaiah was a faithful servant, and he spoke as he was instructed:

- "Woe to you who add house to house and join field to field till no space is left and you live alone in the land" (5:8). Apparently there were those who were guilty of the rape of the land in those days.
- "Woe to those who rise early in the morning to run after their drinks, who stay up late at night till they are inflamed with wine" (5:11).There was evidently a party crowd who needed a word from the Lord.
- "Woe to those who are wise in their own eyes and clever in their own sight" (5:21).

Materialists, party animals and those who suffered from a superiority complex all came under the watchful eye of Adonai and His courageous, outspoken prophet. God had warned them of His displeasure and His intention to bring the consequences of their attitudes and activities on their own heads. The "woe" was a warning. It was also an opportunity to get right with God before the judgment fell.

But a dramatic change took place in Isaiah during his vision. He abruptly stopped preaching "Woe to you" and "Woe to those" and began crying out, "Woe to me!" Instead of arrogantly pronouncing God's general dissatisfaction with the society to which he belonged, Isaiah became excruciatingly aware that he himself was neither immune to the society's ills nor exempt from their woes.

It is always easier to pontificate on the sins of a society as a whole than to confront personal sin. While a case can undoubtedly be made that a corrupt society can be a corrupting influence on the individual, it is equally true that the society which corrupts is not an immaterial entity, but a conglomerate of individuals whose individual sins contribute to the corruption.

The story has been told that *The Times* of London, that elitist newspaper of grand tradition, ran a series of letters to the editor on the subject "What is wrong with the world?" This stimulated great interest over an extended period. Many highly respected people wrote their views, which were duly printed and avidly read by thousands of people. One day a letter appeared from G.K. Chesterton:

> To the Editor, *The Times* of London,
> You ask what is wrong with the world. I am.
> Yours sincerely,
> G.K. Chesterton

Chesterton's brief, witty contribution ended the correspondence. He had hit the nail on the head.

Unclean Lips

Isaiah felt "undone." He sensed he was "ruined," and he was particularly aware that his lips were unclean. If there was one thing Isaiah was known for in his own day, and even down to ours, it was his way with words. His poetry has a beauty and majesty that has survived translation and the passage of time to hold a place among the world's great literature. But suddenly, in the presence of holiness, he was desperately aware that even his strong point was tainted, his greatest gift less than perfect.

He did not specify what he meant by "unclean lips," but he saw a similarity between his problem and that of the society which he described as "a people of unclean lips." We know what they had been saying. Had not Isaiah told them, "Woe to those who call evil good and good evil, who put darkness for light and light for darkness, who put bitter for sweet and sweet for bitter" (5:20)?

Could it be possible that the great Isaiah, when under great social pressure, had changed his message to suit his hearers? Had he "toned down" the word of the Lord even to the point of calling "evil good" and vice versa? We will never know, and we don't need to know, or we would have been told.

But if we are honest with ourselves—and we must be before Holiness—we have to admit our own disconcerting ability to fail at the critical moment. Isaiah had also told them, "Woe to those who draw sin along with cords of deceit, and wickedness as with cart ropes, to those who say, 'Let God hurry, let Him hasten His work so we may see it. Let it approach, let the plan of the Holy One of Israel come so we may know it'" (5:18–19).

Had Isaiah in weak moments joined his unclean lips with those of his compatriots and said this sort of thing? Had he been guilty of deceit? Had he spoken irreverently of God's purposes? Had he carelessly "challenged" God to show His hand? Improbable as it sounds, it was possible that he had misbehaved in this way along with his people. Whatever it was that concerned him, he had no hesitation in confessing it in the ears of the Holy One.

Assuming that Isaiah had been behaving in some ways similar to his contemporaries, it is highly likely that when his conscience pricked him, he was able to quiet it by the all-too-common rationale "Everybody's doing it!" It would have been possible to "dwell among a people of unclean lips" and become so accustomed to the prevailing atmosphere as to be unable to recognize its polluting influence. Urban dwellers who live and breathe in smog may not notice how thick it is until they go up to the mountains and look down upon their polluted city.

"Woe to me!" cried the prophet. He had climbed the mountain, seen the Lord and seen himself. Such was the depth of his cry of contrition that one of the seraphim flew promptly to his aid. His lips, the problem area in which his sin reigned and his guilt was most evident, were touched with a burning coal from the altar. The Holy One was not so removed as to be remote. His holiness did not make Him heartless. Provision had already been made at His initiative to deal with those who are distraught with guilt and in need of grace. Isaiah's sin was cleansed, his guilt removed, and a new dimension of life began.

Here Am I

The Holy One spoke and Isaiah heard. The question asked was, "Who will go for us? Whom shall we send?" Isaiah eagerly volunteered, without any idea of where he would go, what he would do, why he would do it and how it could be done. None of those things mattered. He had caught a vision of holiness, sinfulness and forgiveness, and he was now interested solely in usefulness.

If a vision of holiness leads to a sense of sinfulness which in turn seeks and receives forgiveness, the resulting attitude will be a desire for usefulness, which as thousands through the centuries have proved, leads to happiness—real happiness.

PRAYER

Gracious Father, sometimes it's difficult for us to begin to think in these categories, but You clearly expect us to do so. It's embarrassing for us as well, because we're often so satisfied with ourselves, so confident of ourselves, and yet You bring us to reality.

Some of us are so overwhelmed with what other people have done to us that we can't think about anything else. We're overlooking what we've done to You. Some of us are overlooking the fact that we've got what we've got, and we are what we are, because we were greatly helped; and the more we got what we got, and the more we arrived at where we arrived, the more we took the credit for ourselves and ceased to worship You.

Lord, forgive us. Bring us humbly before Your throne, and give us that great sense of gracious forgiveness that will be so powerful in our hearts that we will respond in worship and service, and gladly honor You, for we recognize that is why we were created. Hear our prayers and let our cries ascend unto You, in the name of Christ Jesus our Lord. Amen.

A PERSONAL NOTE FROM JILL

Soon after I became a Christian, I was introduced to the concept of the quiet time. This was a time an individual could schedule on his or her calendar to be alone with God. If I had not been fortunate enough to be instructed in the "how-tos" of such a daily interview with Divinity, I would never have had a clue as to how to spend such privileged minutes!

The girl who led me to faith, however, was well practiced in her own devotional disciplines and was intent on my learning how to have an Isaiah 6 experience on a daily basis. Using Isaiah 6, she gave me a simple, blow-by-blow account of how it should work.

"First, you have to find a time—it will vary each day, per-haps—and a place," she told me. "Put it on your calendar, like everything else. Then make sure you show up!" She gave me a Bible and suggested I start reading the Gospel of Mark. "Fol-low Jesus through the story," she said. "Notice the way He lives. Think about the things He says; watch the crowd that's watching Him. Jot down your impressions in a notebook" (duly supplied along with the new Bible!).

"What do I write?" I asked, wondering about my ability to write down anything earth-shattering.

"Oh, just anything that strikes you," she replied, "an action that challenges you or a remark that makes you angry or sad—anything. What you're doing," she continued, "is 'seeing' God in action and responding to Him."

Isaiah had some sort of mystical vision. He "saw" with an inner eye into outer space. He saw God in His throne room.

As I followed my friend's instructions, I began to understand that when Jesus said to Philip, "Anyone who has seen Me has seen God" (John 14:9, my paraphrase), Philip was "seeing" the same God Isaiah saw. God, in this case, was clothed in human-ity, wrapped up in our flesh and blood, but nevertheless as much God as God can be. To "watch" Him, gaze at Him, look at Him in the Gospels, is a place to begin to "see" God.

I was absolutely enthralled. I couldn't wait to finish class to run to my quiet place—my bedroom—to look again and again and again. As I read through Mark and then the other three Gospels, "I saw the Lord."

The next thing that happened to Isaiah after he had seen the Lord was that he saw himself. As I saw Jesus being patient with His disciples, I "saw" myself being impatient with my friends! When I read about Him caring about little children, I looked with new eyes at the kids I was teaching and at my attitudes. This self-realization led me to many a contrite "Sorry, Lord!" It was hardly a "Woe is me!" response, but it was the modern equivalent! Like Isaiah overcome with the holiness of Jesus Christ, I was undone at my shortcomings (or coming shorts!). In other words, I came apart in grief at my unworthiness. This naturally led my heart to cry out for forgiveness—for the coal, the fire of refining, cleansing power.

As this dialogue developed day after day and night after night, the new things I was finding out were so life-changing, interesting and exciting that I wanted to share them. But with whom?

"Ask God to 'send' you to someone who needs to hear them," advised my friend. "The result of Isaiah's time with God was a request like that!"

"Here am I, send me," He said. And so I asked God to do just the same with me. He was delighted to comply.

Starting to have a personal devotional time need not be a big thing. Start small like I did. You'll find rewards you wouldn't dream possible! You will begin to sense His otherness, your earthiness, and His empowering to make you holy too!

CHAPTER QUESTIONS

1. It's not how a man begins the Christian life that matters but rather how he ends it. King Uzziah began his walk of faith in grand style but ended dismally.

   a. Read Second Chronicles 26.

   b. Can you relate to this? Think about the "good" influences God has used in your life. How did you respond to them? List a few, if it helps.

c. If you were to write a chapter like this about your life history, how would it parallel Uzziah's experience? Or how would it be different?

d. Which verse do you think is the turning point in Uzziah's story? What can you learn from this?

2. Uzziah addresses the God he sees as ADONAI—the one who is the source of absolute standards, yet gives us the chance to choose our actions and the corresponding repercussions.

a. Do you ever do something you know very well is wrong and then gripe about the repercussions? What is the problem with that approach?

b. What should the fact that God has determined the repercussions of your sinful actions (you reap what you sow) do to your lifestyle choices?

3. Think about Isaiah 6:6—"Here am I, send me"—and spend a few moments of reflection on what it means to "go where He wants you to go and say what He wants you to say." If you cannot honestly say you are willing, ask the Lord for a vision of Himself and a change of heart. Try to avoid praying, "Lord, I am willing to go," if all the time you are secretly planning to stay.

4. Pray the lessons you have learned from this chapter for someone else.

3

CALLED TO BE HOLY

Corinth was no mean city. It was known around the world. Oscar Wilde said, "Nothing succeeds like excess"—he would have loved Corinth! That "philosophy" would have suited Corinth to a T. Strategically placed on the narrow isthmus between the Aegean and Adriatic Seas at the intersection of major trade routes, a center of trade and religion, sport and philosophy, culture and decadence, Corinth was a byword. It was brilliant, beautiful, blasé and bad.

With Paul's eye for strategy, he no doubt thought that a church planted in such a world-renowned city would have an impact out of all proportion to its size. So he set to work there, and despite disappointments and depressing circumstances, the church of God in Corinth came into being. Second to none in spiritual gifts and enrichment, the church was, however, a major disappointment. It was torn apart by internal strife, much of which was generated by interlopers who besmirched Paul's reputation, challenged his apostleship, denigrated his message and created havoc in the church he planted and nurtured.

Incredibly blind to its glaring immorality, arrogant and smug beyond belief, this church felt perfectly justified in questioning the authority of Paul, the one who had brought the gospel to Corinth in the first place. He told them quite frankly that he had first approached their city "in weakness and fear, and with much trembling" (1 Cor. 2:3), and much later, after dealing with their problems, he confessed that he wrote to them "out of great distress and anguish of heart and with many tears" (2 Cor. 2:4).

This wicked city, full of vast potential, desperately needed a church that would testify in word and deed to the life-transforming power of the gospel. In the midst of corruption and decadence, there was a crying need for righteousness and integrity. The streets, full of people living in darkness, needed to ring with the powerful message of the living Lord. But sadly, this church was more committed to self-destructing than truth-declaring; as a result, the opportunities presented were being missed, the message muted and the divinely ordained mandate largely unfulfilled. There was obviously something rotten in the state of the Corinthian church.

Sanctified in Christ Jesus

In light of the problems in this church in general, and in its dealings with Paul in particular, it is surprising to hear him addressing them as "those sanctified in Christ Jesus." The word sanctified is closely related to "holy," "separate" and "saint." So he was in effect calling them saints—holy people!

Some people believe that a saint is an unusual individual who, having lived an extraordinary life and performed verifiable miracles, is recognized officially by the church—people like St. Patrick and St. Augustine. Others use the term more loosely to identify someone of gracious demeanor with a capacity for end-less patience, as in "To have put up with him for all these years, she must be a saint!" But the way Paul described the Corinthians hardly meets either of these uses. They were certainly not saints in either sense of the word.

To be sanctified means that something or someone has been "set apart" by God for a specific purpose. It is something God does. The Corinthians were sanctified because they had been placed in a position where they had gained a new status. This position was "in Christ"—a favorite expression of Paul's. His meaning was perfectly clear to the Corinthians: "God chose the foolish things of the world to shame the wise; God chose the weak things of the world to shame the strong. . . . It is because of him that you are in Christ Jesus" (1 Cor. 1:27, 30). They were "in Christ Jesus" because of God's call on their lives, and this call had come to them at His initiative.

Also, His call had been stimulated by His grace and not by their worth. God had not gone round Corinth looking for top dogs well known for their outstanding credentials and achieve-ments. On the contrary, He had carefully taken initiatives in the lives of those who frankly didn't amount to much in the normal reckoning.

He reasoned that if a group of outstanding people "got re-ligion" or became spiritually outstanding, the watching world would write off their religion as singularly unremarkable. A jad-ed public, well accustomed to new lifestyles and exotic develop-ments, would see it as nothing more than outstanding people being outstanding! But if a group of no-names, apparently de-void of resources or unusual abilities, began to do outstanding things, people would be curious and on inquiry might recognize that God was at work and give Him the glory.

God has consistently operated in this way. Right from the beginning of His dealings with Israel, He made it painfully clear that He had not chosen them because they were special. On the contrary, they were outstanding only in their mediocrity. When missionaries first went into Ethiopia, God did not direct them to the proud ruling Amharas, but to the slaves of the Wollamo tribe. But the Wollamos served in all the wealthy families, and so the message made its way into all echelons of society through the despised class.

More recently there are reports that some Saudi Arabian officials are concerned because the children of elite Islamic families are learning more about Jesus than about the Prophet, because Christian Filipino maids who care for the children are teaching them the gospel. God has always taken great delight in calling the unlikely to do the improbable. But the key is that ordinary people, whether Wollamo, Filipino or Corinthian, must recognize that they were set apart for a divine purpose, and then must commit themselves to that end.

Understanding the Corinthians

Having received the call, the Corinthians had responded and found themselves "in Christ," that is, related to Christ in such a way that He had become for them their "righteousness, holiness, and redemption" (1 Cor. 1:30). In order to understand what God had done in placing them in Christ, it is helpful to remember what they were into before God placed them in Christ. The more we are acquainted with their former condition, the more able we are to appreciate their new status.

It is generally true that we can better recognize what a person is if we understand what he was. The exploits of Paul, magnificent as they are in themselves, are seen to be even greater when we remember he used to be Saul the persecutor. The preaching of Peter at Pentecost, powerful as it undoubtedly was, assumes greater magnificence when we remember that he was previously Simon of the triple denials. But what had these Corinthian Christians been getting into before Christ? What kind of people were they?

The Jews

There were Greeks and Jews in Corinth, and their lifestyles differed dramatically. When Paul arrived in Corinth, he went along to the synagogue and began to preach Christ to the assembled company. First they were intrigued by his message, but eventually they were "scandalized." In a way, this is understandable. They reasoned as follows:

1. The Scriptures state "Cursed is everyone who hangs on a tree";
2. Jesus of Nazareth was hanged on a tree (crucified);
3. therefore, Jesus was accursed;
4. Messiah cannot be accursed;
5. therefore, Jesus is not the Messiah (Christ).
6. Moreover, it is a scandal that this man, Paul, should be teaching this heresy in our synagogue.

As a result, people in the synagogue rejected Paul and his message. He became *persona non grata*. In addition, the Jews insisted on seeing miraculous signs before they would believe anything. And they reserved the right to decide if the sign was miraculous enough for their liking.

There was nothing new about this. The day after Jesus fed the five thousand with five loaves and two fishes, and had twelve baskets of crumbs left over, their totally skeptical response was, "What miraculous sign then will you give that we may see it and believe you?" (John 6:30). "Big deal" was their attitude!

In Paul's day they demanded "signs," but they were not willing to accept the sign of the Resurrection as clear evidence that Jesus was indeed the Christ and had become accursed for them, to deliver them from the curse of the law. They were sticking to their either/or argument: He can't be Christ and also be cursed—it's one or the other! They refused point-blank to accept the Resurrection as evidence that it was both/and—He was both Christ and cursed. Their arrogance and independence had left them far from the kingdom.

But not all of them. Crispus and his household, Sosthenes and many others "believed and were baptized" (Acts 18:8). When these Corinthian Jews were confronted with the message that Messiah must of necessity be accursed for them by dying on a tree, they became aware of their own sinfulness. Instead of priding themselves that they had kept the letter of the law and were righteous—that their Jewishness guaranteed their righteousness—they became aware of the extent to which they had broken the spirit of the law.

They were experts at stretching the law without breaking it, getting around it without trampling over it, going through the motions while knowing little of the motive of loving God. Paul's ministry was a dreadful eye opener for them, and they recognized their unrighteousness. Having failed to establish their own righteousness, and as a result having discovered their unrighteousness, they were ready to hear about Jesus who had become their righteousness.

They were eagerly open to hearing how they could be declared righteous, undeservedly and unreservedly, by God as a gift, having failed to be so declared on the basis of merit. Paul showed how God through Christ would make them right with Him, despite the fact that they had endeavored to do it themselves and had finished up decidedly "unright" with Him.

Baptized into Christ and discovering Him as their righteousness, they also found themselves "sanctified in Christ Jesus"—set apart for Him and His service. He had become their "righteousness, holiness, and redemption." They could not pick and choose; they could not get excited about Christ being their righteousness and blissfully ignore that He was therefore their sanctification and would finally be their redemption. They were not free to embrace the wonders of being declared righteous while at the same time avoiding the call to holiness—their new status as set apart for God's purposes.

The Greeks

You can't ignore the Greeks. The influence of Aristotle and Plato, Euclid and Archimedes, to name a few, is felt today even in the lives of people who know so little about them that they think they played for the Athens rugby team! They were great thinkers, and this was both their strength and their weakness. Paul, who was no stranger to Greek culture, knew that they had developed carefully reasoned philosophies upon which they were building their lives:

- The Stoics believed that the world was managed by a rational but impersonal force. Since they couldn't beat this force, they had prudently decided to join it and let whatever would be, be. They lived by the Hellenistic equivalent of "Que sera, sera." In this way, they expected to find a measure of peace and contentment.

- The Epicureans, on the other hand, were of the opinion that life's events are the result of atoms colliding with each other purely by chance. So the thing to do was to hope that your luck would hold out as long as possible and that you would be somewhere else when the atoms collided; in the meantime, the thing to do was to "eat, drink, and be merry."

Professor F.F. Bruce comments, "Stoicism and Epicureanism represent alternative attempts in pre-Christian paganism to come to terms with life . . . and post-Christian paganism down to our own day has not been able to devise anything appreciably better."[6] The Stoics opted for fate and the Epicureans for chance; neither were open to Paul's personal God, the Holy One, whose Son had died and risen again. They contemptuously dismissed his message from their lofty philosophical perches.

But not all! There were some in whose lives the gospel made dramatic changes. Paul exclaimed, "Brothers, think of what you were when you were called" (1 Cor. 1:26). There were not a few Greeks who, instead of dismissing the message of the cross as foolishness, recognized the repercussions of their philosophies in terms of broken lives and turned to Christ, and in so doing were made "righteous" and "sanctified."

So there were both Jews and Greeks who came from unrighteous lifestyles and found Christ to be their "righteousness, sanctification, and redemption." To these new Christians, Paul insisted, "Do you not know that the wicked [unrighteous] will not inherit the kingdom of God? Do not be deceived" (1 Cor. 6:9). The word unrighteous is significant. Those whose philosophical premises are not right do not, cannot, live rightly—they are unrighteous. In the same way, those whose religion is based on erroneous doctrines develop an ethic that is in error and a lifestyle that is unrighteous. The penalty for unrighteous living is banishment from the kingdom of God. The manifestations of unrighteousness are plain to see. They fall into three main categories: immorality, idolatry and indulgence. The history of the children of Israel was littered with examples of all three and the Greek lifestyle even more so.

Paul told the Corinthians that most of them were not very noble, wise or influential (he left out "not very beautiful!") and that many of them had been involved in the immoral, indulgent and idolatrous lifestyles of their culture. But then he added, "You were washed, you were sanctified, you were justified in the name of the Lord Jesus and by the Spirit of our God" (1 Cor. 6:11).

The washing, sanctifying and justifying had taken place in them because Christ had become "righteousness, holiness, and redemption" for them. What He had provided for them through His death and resurrection had been applied to them by the Spirit of God, who had convicted them of the error in their thinking and the unrighteousness of their living. He had opened their eyes to "the foolishness of what was preached"—the gospel had made available to them the cleansing from sin and the inflowing of life which placed them in Christ, and credited to them all His merits while canceling out all their demerits. They were different, set apart, something else—holy!

When Isaiah recognized his cleansing, he promptly offered himself for service, and was immediately put to work. In similar fashion the Corinthians were "set apart" for God's glory. It cannot be stressed too much to modern Christians, who have often been won to Christ because of the great attractiveness of His blessings, that in the act of being justified and redeemed they are also being set apart. One could sometimes gain the impression from faulty preaching or selective hearing that the sanctified part of the gospel can be separated from the justified part, without in any way diminishing the message. The idea that you can be saved without being sanctified ignores half the message and totally misses the point.

In the world of professional sports, this would be like an athlete signing a large contract, receiving the payment, but seeing no necessity to play for the team, turn up for practice, attend team meetings or even wear the club uniform. And then assuming he has the right, if he wishes, to play for the opposing team! This would be unthinkable, of course, because once he signs on, he is "sanctified" to the new team—set apart for them.

Called to Be Holy

Jill and I got married because we loved each other very much and wanted to spend the rest of our lives together. Convinced that being together would greatly enrich our lives, we had no doubts that we would live happily ever after and that this state of marital bliss would be mutually advantageous.

With these thoughts filling our hearts and minds, we duly presented ourselves at the church on time. The minister, after a few appropriate remarks and a few hymns, finally got down to business. He required us to make a commitment that we would take each other "For better, for worse, for richer, for poorer, in sickness and in health, till death do us part."

But there was another little phrase that was most significant, although it is not as well known. We were each to promise not only to take each other but to keep ourselves "only for each other." There was an exclusivity about the commitment as well as an exuberance. There were great benefits stretching away to the horizon, but there was great limitation too. To take each other was a blessing; to keep ourselves for each other was a mandate.

These two were bound up together. To experience the untold delights of having someone love you to eternity requires from you a corresponding commitment.

But our wedding vows were obviously more than a ceremonial statement. They were a commitment full of the most practical considerations. There was to be no abandoning of the other if sickness made a sickening invasion, no deserting of the other if things got worse instead of better, and absolutely no trading in of the contract if poverty took over from riches.

As soon as I had made my wedding vows and the minister pronounced Jill and me "husband and wife," I recognized that I was now a married man. But when I had time to reflect on my new status, I knew that I knew very little about being a married man. My status was clear—I had a certificate to prove it. My behavior now had to catch up.

So for more than fifty years, my wife, a trained teacher, has been instructing me in a personal seminar entitled "How to be married now that you are" or alternatively, "Learning to be what you have become!" In other words, we have been working out the practical behavioral details of our status as married people. For status is one thing, but behavior related to status is another.

"Sanctified in Christ Jesus" (which is status) leads to "called to be holy" (which is behavior). The former tells us what we became; the latter speaks of what we are to be.

The Call of God

We need to focus on the critical word "call." For God to call a person means that He offers an opportunity. It is an invitation from God Himself to an undeserving person. The invitation is to participate in the unique experience that God has prepared. But because the call originates with God, it resonates with His authority and therefore includes a sense of summons. On the one hand, God graciously extends an opportunity—an invitation. On the other hand, He does so in an authoritative manner which requires our obedient response. This means that when the call is received, it is to be treated with great respect and appreciation.

When Queen Elizabeth holds one of her garden parties at Buckingham Palace, some people are surprised to receive invitations. They never expected such an opportunity, and they regard it as an unusual privilege. They will have the chance to actually meet the Queen and go to her house. The fact that there will be 2,000 other people there, or that they won't get inside her house, doesn't seem very important at the time. Should they choose to accept the invitation, they will receive specific instructions concerning what they should wear, when they should arrive and where they should present themselves. They will be reminded that it is appropriate for men to bow and women to curtsy (which Nancy Reagan refused to do on principle!) to the Queen, and that court etiquette requires that they speak to Her Majesty only after they have been spoken to.

For some people who are not too excited about royalty, these requirements may be more than they bargained for. They may have no objection to attending a nice garden party with some movers and shakers, but all this etiquette business is a bit too much. That leaves them a couple of options: either they choose not to attend or they swallow hard and meet the conditions.

Notice that there is no third option. They are not free to show up late, dressed in blue jeans and T-shirt, or to slap the Queen on the back and say, "Hi, Liz! How ya doin'?" They have certainly received an invitation, but there is an element of summons to it as well. They were invited—but with limits! On her terms, not their own. So it is with the divine call.

It is sometimes not adequately understood what is included in the divine call. For instance, when some people read, "God, who has called you into fellowship with His Son Jesus Christ our Lord, is faithful" (1 Cor. 1:9), they could think that the call of God is an invitation to enjoy a relationship with His Son—and nothing more. It would be a serious mistake to assume that the call of God is solely a generous offer from God for undeserving people to have a nice time with Jesus. The invitation is also a summons. By all means, rejoice in the fellowship to be enjoyed with the Lord Jesus, but not at the expense of ignoring the summons to live a holy life without which the fellowship would not be real and true.

There is no freedom for individuals to go to God's garden party other than on the conditions He outlined, and these include the call to be holy. Living a holy life is no more an optional extra for the "called" than is behaving appropriately for those who respond to the royal invitation. In responding to the call, accepting the invitation, there is an acknowledgement of what is involved.

Much confusion concerning Christian living could and would be avoided if this were made clear. Those who are being invited to "receive Christ" should be rightly informed as to the ramifications of so doing. Those who have made a commitment to Him, but unfortunately have not been instructed concerning their calling, must be informed. Those whose lives are spent ineffectually need to be encouraged to explore the meaning of a "set apart" life. And those who, out of spiritual boredom, spend their time in the spiritual shallows, deserve to be introduced to the depth of experience to which they have already been called. It's a lot to be humble about.

The Corinthians who responded to the message and heard

the call began to exhibit a holy lifestyle in essentially practical ways. The Greeks among them were well known for their intelligence. They had spent a lot of time being philosophical only to reason themselves into something of a philosophical dead end. Their initial reaction to the message of God's Son, with particular reference to His incarnation and subsequent death and resurrection, had been to dismiss it as philosophically untenable.

But as Paul reasoned with them and the message took root in their thinking, they began to see that their "wisdom" looked pretty foolish, and what they had regarded it as "foolish" appeared to be the wisdom of God. This was a very humbling experience for all concerned, and particularly for intelligent, sophisticated people who had been convinced they had all the right answers to all the correct questions!

The essential message that they were sinners who were incapable of redeeming themselves struck deeply into the pride of those who looked with great admiration upon themselves and their accomplishments. Big people began to look small when standing alongside Christ, and smart people didn't look half so smart when confronted with the errors of their thinking and the spiritual darkness in which they lived.

Once humbled, they learned to stay that way. As they progressed in the spiritual life, they learned on a daily basis how frail they were and how wrong they could be. Instead of arrogant assumptions of self-sufficiency, they learned humble submission to divine authority. The change was dramatic. It was evidence of a newness of life—a setting apart, a holy lifestyle.

Winston Churchill had a distinct distaste for his political opponent Clement Attlee. But on one occasion he surprised some people by admitting that Attlee was a very humble man. He quickly added however, "Of course, he has a lot to be humble about." So do we all. The extent to which we express it so often determines the reality of a holy life.

PRAYER

Lord, we recognize the immensity of Your self-revelation and as a result we recognize the inadequacy of our own selves before You. Without Your grace we're lost. But how grateful we are that in Your goodness You gave Christ on the cross—and in so doing, You've made the wisdom of man foolishness.

How dare people think that they can dictate terms to You? How dare they think that life is just a matter of luck or a matter of chance or a matter of cold unrelenting fate, when You have revealed Yourself in Christ to be a deeply holy and an incredibly personal God?

Lord, teach us to respond to You by manifesting the fact that Christ has become our righteousness, our holiness and our redemption, for we pray in Christ's name. Amen.

A PERSONAL NOTE FROM JILL

I once had an old spinster aunt, a great-aunt, who lived alone in a small house in England. As was the custom in our country, the homes were heated by a single coal fire in the living room— or parlor, as it was called. My great-aunt lived and moved and had her being in this cozy little room.

The day came when she bought her first television set. What a wonder it was! For a lady born in the late 1800s, who had seen the horse and trap replaced by the motor car, it was a miracle! She moved her bed into the parlor and became quite addicted to the 10 p.m. news and the nice man who read it to her. He seemed to be speaking right to her from her "miracle box." He became a friend—her company. This was a fine way to finish the day.

There was one thing my old aunt could never bring herself to do. She could never bring herself to get undressed in front of the TV set if her new friend—that nice man—was reading the news and looking at her! Such modesty was both touching and humorous to my sister and me.

"Why, he can't see you, Auntie," I teased her.

"I know, I know," she replied, "but I still don't feel it's quite 'nice.'"

Many years later I knelt by my bed in my own little bedroom. I had just come to Christ, and it was all new. My life had been so awfully empty and messed up, and then someone had told me about Christ's love for me, and how He had died to save me. I opened my Bible and began to read about a holy God who had purer eyes than could bear to look on evil. And then I read the verse that said, "Nothing in all creation is hidden from God's sight. Everything is uncovered and laid bare before the eyes of Him to whom we must give account" (Heb. 4:13).

Suddenly, I was a little girl again, laughing at my old auntie refusing to get undressed in front of her television set. Now I knew how she felt! But this time it wasn't pieces of cloth that were the issue but the very wrappings of my soul. And this wasn't about a man who was speaking from a studio somewhere miles away, but about a God who sees right through the glad rags of our trivial lifestyles and lays bare exactly who we are. He could see it all!

There was nowhere to run and nowhere to hide. I couldn't turn the television off or clothe myself suitably so I wouldn't be ashamed. All things were exposed. Not some things but all things. I was overcome with guilt and shame. Yet, somehow, I managed to read on in my Bible that day until I dared to lift up my eyes to meet His. It was only a swift saving glance upward, but it was enough. I couldn't look away, for there, in the holy eyes of God, was a tear. I was so, so sorry for the sin—and so was He! When God looks at us, He sees everything He has died for. That's why there are tears in His eyes.

CHAPTER QUESTIONS

1. Read First Corinthians 1:26–31. God chooses to draw people to Himself.

   a. How would you describe them?

   b. Which adjective would best describe you?

   c. What does this do to your personal pride?

2. The Corinthians' conversion was dramatic. They went from being very bad to being quite good. Do you ever wish you had a personal experience that you could look back on that was as dramatic as theirs? Do you ever secretly wish you had such a conversion so you could be more excited about Christ than you are? Yet the Bible speaks of a commonality of our sinful state before conversion that has nothing to do with the "degree" of sinfulness.

   a. Read Isaiah 64:6 and meditate on it.

   b. What does this verse say to you? Is it hard to honestly believe?

   c. Ask God to help you see yourself as God sees you.

   d. Read First Corinthians 6:11 and spend time praising God for what He has done for you.

3. Read the illustration of the athlete described at the end of the section on "The Greeks." Write an honest description of your "athletic performance" as a Christian. It could start, "I occasionally turn up for Sunday practice (if there's nothing good on TV)," etc.

4. Did someone lead you to Christ, or did you find Him yourself? If someone led you to the Lord, did they tell you that you would be required to live a holy lifestyle? If you found the Lord yourself, when did you come to the realization that justification should lead to sanctification? Write a paragraph that expresses your understanding of sanctification.

5. If we measure ourselves by Christ, we keep ourselves in perspective. Read First Corinthians 13. Then reread verses 4–6. These verses describe the life of love that Christ lived. How do you measure up?

6. Spend some time in prayer about living a holy life.

4

Be Holy Because I Am Holy

Therefore, prepare your minds for action; be self-controlled; set your hope fully on the grace to be given you when Jesus Christ is revealed. As obedient children, do not conform to the evil desires you had when you lived in ignorance. But just as He who called you is holy, so be holy in all you do; for it is written: "Be holy, because I am holy." (1 PET. 1:13–16)

Jim was a big fellow who stood out in any crowd without try-ing. As I saw him standing alone—and rather ill at ease—in church, I went to him and introduced myself. His face bright-ened as I approached him, and he said, "I've only just started coming here, but it's great. And all these talks you give are great. You're telling us all about the people in the Bible, and I love hearing about them."

"What is it about these stories that you enjoy so much?" I inquired.

Without hesitation he replied, "Oh, I love hearing about these guys because they're all worse than me!" (I was preaching in the Old Testament at the time and realized he had been finding some comfort in the stories of rascals like Jacob and drunks like Noah.)

I have found a similar reaction among men when I've taught about some of the people in the New Testament as well—Simon Peter for instance. Men often tell me, "I like Peter because I can relate to him. He messed up and so do I." There is no doubt that the Bible does nothing to hide Simon Peter's flaws from us, but in all fairness to him, we need to point out that this flawed man became a "Rock" through the gracious working of Jesus through the Spirit in his life. So much so that in his later days he was able to speak convincingly to the people about the call of God on their lives, and they listened because they could see the reality of God's work in him.

Peter was able to make a very strong plea to Christians concerning their lifestyles. He called people to holiness of life. And he said that we are to be holy for the very simple reason that the One who called us is holy. God told His people, "Be holy because I am holy."

He Who Is Holy Has Provided for Us Redemption

Now Peter didn't dream this up himself. He was quoting from the Book of Leviticus, which recorded for the children of Israel (and for our benefit too) the instructions concerning their lifestyle in their new environment, given to them in the wilderness en route from the bondage of Egypt to the freedom of the Promised Land.

Basically He said, "Now listen, I have redeemed you and I am holy, and you now belong to Me. I have chosen you to be My people, and accordingly, I have some expectations of you. They are simple and basic and can be summarized this way: 'Because I am holy, you are to live holy lives.'"

Peter took this picture and applied it to Christians. He said, "In the same way that the children of Israel were in bondage in Egypt and God set them free, liberated them, redeemed them, so men and women today are in bondage, and God in Christ is prepared to set them free."

Some people object to any suggestion that they might be in bondage to anything. There's nothing new about that! One day Jesus told some of his disciples, "The truth will set you free." They replied indignantly, "We have never been slaves of anyone. How can you say that we shall be set free?" Jesus' retort was brief and to the point, "Everyone who sins is a slave to sin" (John 8:32–34).

"Everyone who sins," however decent, law-abiding and respectable they may be, is demonstrating that they are fallen— that is, they are considerably less than they were created to be and therefore fall short of the divine standards and intentions. The results of this "shortfall" we call sin; the consequence is spiritual alienation, a kind of death. It's as if the nerve of the God/human relationship has been severed, resulting in emptiness, lostness, confusion and aimlessness. Or as Paul explained it, "The wages of sin is death" (Rom. 6:23).

There is nothing that a human being can do about this situation, but God in Christ can and did. Christ died our death (assumed the consequences of our fall) and offers us new life, free from these consequences. Moreover, He rose again and offers us His resurrection life so that we can live progressively free (and freer) from the debilitating effects of sin. Free indeed! Redeemed!

But remember that the One who sets us free, who redeems us, in so doing bought us for Himself. And He is a holy God. It follows, therefore, that because He is holy, He expects us to live a holy life.

My dad used to tell the story of a little boy who built a model sailing boat and took it out on the ocean. A gust of wind caught it and swept it out to sea. He was understandably upset about this. Sometime later the little boy was walking past a toy shop. He looked in the window, and there was his boat!

He went inside and said to the man who owned the store, "That's my boat you've got in your window."

The man replied, "No, son, you're mistaken. But it will be yours if you buy it."

So he rushed home and said, "Dad, they've got my boat in the toy store window, and I want it back."

His father went with him to the store and said, "That is my son's boat. He lost it when he was sailing it one day. Is there any way we can have it back?"

The store owner said, "Yes, if you buy it."

So being a good dad, he got out his wallet, paid the money and gave the boat to his son who, clutching it to his chest, said, "This is my boat twice. Once because I made it and twice because I bought it." Now that's one way of looking at redemption.

God made us for Himself but, unfortunately, we went our own way. We were swept out to sea by all kinds of winds and currents, and got away from Him. He wanted to get us back because He'd made us; and so His Son, Jesus, died on the cross and paid the price to set us free so that we could belong to Him. It's as if God is saying to us, "You're mine twice, once because I made you and twice because I redeemed you."

When we begin to understand this, it stimulates within us a desire to be the people that God wants us to be. That's how the desire to live a holy life begins to work. Now granted, if we were asked, "Which would you rather be: happy, healthy or holy?" we might be more interested in being happy and healthy. But God clearly calls us to be holy people—not that He is disinterested in our health and happiness!

But there is still more that we need to grasp about redemption. For instance, Peter said that we were redeemed from "the empty way of life handed down to you from your forefathers" (1 Pet. 1:18). Is it true that sometimes we develop a lifestyle that is based on the one handed down to us, and that we develop it without seriously considering what life is all about? I think so. There is often a tendency for us to emulate unthinkingly and uncritically the examples of people who have gone on before us. We simply buy into what they've done and we live as they lived.

A newly married young lady decided to boil a ham. As they hadn't been married very long, the husband went into the kitchen to see what she was doing. He was rather surprised to see that she cut both ends off the ham before putting it in the pan, so he asked, "Why did you do that?"

She said, "Because that's how you boil a ham."

"Well, where did you get that idea from?" he inquired.

She replied, "My mother taught me how to do this."

So he went to see his mother-in-law and asked her, "How do you boil a ham?"

She said, "You cut both ends off the ham, put it in a pan, and you boil it. My mother always did it this way."

The next time he saw Grandma he inquired of her, "Do you cut both ends off the ham before you boil it?"

"Yes I do," she responded.

"But why?" he asked.

She said, "Because my pan isn't big enough."

"But why do you cut a piece off both ends of the ham?" He asked.

"Because my pan is not big enough at both ends."

Many traditions are born of circumstances which were either initially misunderstood or are no longer relevant. These traditions are then eagerly adopted into contemporary lifestyles, frequently without critical evaluation. Lifestyles based on things handed down from forefathers—or foremothers—might, on a closer look, be seen to be "an empty way of life."

That would be bad enough, but Peter goes on to explain that we also tend to "conform to the evil desires" that are the result of "ignorance" (1:14). Now if we copy an example without thinking and are susceptible to "evil desire" and "ignorance" of spiritual truth, it is not hard to imagine the mess we may make of life.

Some of us, in fact, don't have to imagine. We can look at our lives and say, "I never really understood how I got myself into this mess, but now I do. I never bothered to think. I lived in ignorance of spiritual principles and simply gave in to evil desires and copied the way people all around me lived. No wonder my life is so empty!" The good news, of course, is that God intends to redeem us from that kind of bondage. That is what we are redeemed from.

But in addition to being redeemed *from* we are redeemed *by* God being merciful to us. There is no other reason we could ever be reconciled to a holy God. If God had not decided to do it, it would not have been done. And the basis on which it was accomplished, as Peter explained, is not silver or gold or any perishable thing, but the cross of Christ, the shed blood of the Lord Jesus. Now this is the point. When I begin to understand what I am redeemed from and who I am redeemed by, I discover the enormity of redemption and discern a desire to live differently.

This leads to another consideration, and that is, what have I been redeemed for? Peter lists a number of things. He says,

"Since you call on a Father who judges each man's work impartially . . ." (1:17). The word "Father" suggests family. As He has become our Father, we have become members of His family. Accordingly, we begin to find our identity in relationship with the Father and in the context of the family of God. This is what we have been redeemed for.

In this family we have been "born again into a living hope" (1:3). We have been given an "inheritance that can never perish" (1:4). And the net result, ultimately, will be "the salvation of our souls" (1:9). All these things bear looking into, because we have been redeemed from an old lifestyle by the mercy of God and the blood of Christ unto newness of life. And it is He who is holy who has provided this redemption for us.

He Who Has Provided Redemption Has Outlined His Requirements

What are the requirements He outlines for us? The answer is to be found throughout both the Old and New Testaments. He who is holy has redeemed us, and His requirement is that we should live holy lives.

But why? Isn't this an unreasonable expectation on God's part? Not at all, and there are two specific reasons for that.

The first reason is that He is the One who has invited us to become related to Him—we did not invite ourselves! If you join the army, you're given a uniform and you wear it proudly. What would you think of somebody who joined the army and wore the uniform of the enemy? You would say, "He's a traitor."

What would you say if somebody who had been redeemed insisted on living a life totally contrary to the requirements of the holy God? There's a sense in which that could be called spiritual treason. He who is holy has called us to wear the uniform of His holiness.

The second reason is that He has called us to live a life of holiness. First Thessalonians 4:7 puts it quite clearly: "God did not call us to be impure, but to live a holy life." In other words, what He had in mind when He redeemed us from the old life was not simply to forgive us and take us to heaven when we die. When He redeemed us from the old life, it was for newness of life on the way to heaven, and the new life is to be characterized by holiness. God had holiness in mind for us all along.

We need to underline this because frequently people think that you simply come to God through Christ to have your sins forgiven so that life can become reasonably comfortable. You get all the wrinkles taken out and then live pretty much as you want, and when you die, you go to heaven. But the overriding concern of a holy God is that He should call out a holy people who are characterized by a life of holiness.

Now it's one thing to say that, and it's an entirely different thing to know how in the world to achieve it. Peter gives us three very helpful instructions in First Peter 1:13:

1. "Therefore, prepare your minds for action."
2. "Be self-controlled."
3. "Set your hope fully on the grace to be given you when Jesus Christ is revealed."

These are three practical requirements for developing a holy lifestyle—and I use the term "lifestyle" advisedly, deriving it from the Greek word *anastrophe*. Peter was so fond of this word that he used it eight times in his epistles. In our English version the word is translated in a variety of ways, such as: "all you do" (1:15); "empty way of life" (1:18); "live such good lives" (2:12). In modern English anastrophe means "lifestyle." We are to avoid

an empty lifestyle and adopt a holy lifestyle which even unbelievers will hopefully find attractive.

Some people have the impression that holiness is something
you put on when you go to church. You live a normal life, and
then on Sunday morning you put on holiness for a brief hour
while it is refurbished; then you stow it away carefully before
reentering the real world. But holiness is not an awkward ap-
pendage to normal life or a retreat into a monastic way of life.
The whole point is that holiness is to be an integral part of real
daily living. Holiness shows "in all you do" (1:15).

A Well-Ordered Mind

Peter's three instructions are very helpful. First of all, "Prepare
your minds for action" (1:13). The expression that he uses reminds
us of the children of Israel being redeemed from Egypt. They were
told that they would need to get out of Egypt in a hurry, and so
they were told to "gird up their loins." That is the expression that
Peter uses; he told his readers, "Gird up the loins of your mind."
Let me explain. The best way to keep cool in the baking heat of
the Middle East is to wear long, loose, flowing cotton robes. But
they're not very good for getting anywhere in a hurry. If you have
to flee from Egypt (or catch an overcrowded subway train in Cai-
ro), you gird up your loins, which means that you bend down, get
hold of the bottom of your garment, hike it up between your legs,
hitch the loose ends into your belt, and take off.

Peter says, "Do the same thing with your mind. There are a
lot of loose ends in your thinking. There's a lot of stuff cluttering
up your mind. So what you really need is a well-ordered mind
if you are to develop a holy lifestyle." How will this work? "As
obedient children, do not conform to the evil desires you had
when you lived in ignorance" (1:14). One of the things that

we need to get firmly into our minds is that if we have been re-deemed by the Holy One, and He has become our Father, then our relationship to Him must be that of an obedient child to a holy, heavenly Father.

One of the interesting things that happens when I talk or write on this subject is that people say to me, "Stuart, be careful that in your emphasis on the holiness and the righteousness of God that you don't get away from the fatherhood of God. There are so many hurting people who need to be reminded of God being a loving Father."

To that I reply that I understand the necessity for balance here—and you'll find it in the Bible in verses such as First Peter 1:17: "Since you call on a Father who judges each man's work impartially, live your lives as strangers here in reverent fear." You can't drive a wedge between the holiness and the righteousness of God on the one hand and the fatherhood of God on the other. He is a loving, caring, gracious, merciful Father who disciplines and judges His children. It's all together. I've got to get my mind firmly fixed on the idea that I am now the child of the heavenly Father who expects me to live in obedience.

Obedience is not a very popular word. I vividly remember my father talking to me about obedience when I was small. Before he disciplined me, he always said something that puzzled me: "Stuart, this is going to hurt me more than it will hurt you."

I remember thinking, *Dad, please don't hurt yourself. I don't want you to do that.*

But now that I have been both a father and a grandfather for many years, I know that loving fathers discipline, loving fathers judge, loving fathers expect obedience—and not out of malevolence or because they enjoy inflicting pain. If I'm going to develop a holy lifestyle, my mind must be set on obedience to my heavenly Father—a lesson He is committed to teaching me.

Peter also said, "Live your lives as strangers here in reverent fear" (1:17). And he wrote about our being "aliens and strangers in the world" (2:11). Our mind-set is to be that of people who live in an alien culture.

One day in Haiti I got into a discussion on culture, and somebody said, "We've been discussing culture, but nobody has defined it." A Haitian lady physician who had studied in the USA said, "Culture is that which makes you uncomfortable when you're away from home." I thought that was a rather interesting definition. When you move away from home, you're uncomfortable because the values, customs, priorities and behavior patterns differ from those at home, and you don't know where you fit or how to respond.

If we're to live as aliens and strangers in this world, we've got to understand that this world has a culture which at times is contrary to the holiness of God. Our problem is that we are far too much at home in this culture and have not developed the attitude of aliens and strangers. A holy lifestyle may require me to move around in the culture of which I'm a part, saying, "I recognize that my prime responsibility is to live in obedience to my heavenly Father. If what He says is contrary to what my culture expects, condones or encourages, then I will live in obedience to Him, and I will accept the fact that I'm a misfit in my culture." It's all part of developing a holy lifestyle, and it comes from a well-ordered mind.

A Well-Disciplined Lifestyle

The second instruction is to be "self-controlled" or "sober." The Greek word Peter used was related directly to alcohol. In our society, regardless of what the compelling beer advertisers are saying, we know that alcohol abuse is an absolute scourge. It is devastating our youth, our families and our society. It is a scandal, and it is imperative that Christians have their minds clear on this point and discipline themselves accordingly. However, when Scripture says to be "self-controlled" or "sober," it is not limiting itself to alcohol abuse. It is talking about all areas of life in which we surrender our abilities to things that are contrary to God.

We need to develop well-disciplined lifestyles and be willing, if necessary, to be nonconformists. We need to demonstrate self-controlled abstinence when appropriate. Nancy Reagan told us, "Just say no." She was on the right track, but she didn't go far enough. It is one thing to tell people, "Just say no," but it's an entirely different thing to tell them *why* they should and *how* to do it. The Christian can explain both the why and the how of the disciplined life. The reason we say no to certain things is because they are contrary to the holiness of God and are detrimental to a life of holiness.

Some people get nervous when you talk like this because it seems so negative. But note the balancing positive. Peter said that if you live as obedient children, as aliens and strangers, and abstain from sinful desires which war against the soul, you will live "such good lives among the pagans that, even though they accuse you of doing wrong, they may see your good deeds and glorify God" (2:12).

One of the results of a holy lifestyle is that while some people will be irritated by you and critical of you, they will be confronted by the sheer goodness that results from your lifestyle and the blessing that flows from your life. They will not all give God the glory, but many will. It's tough being an odd-ball or a misfit, but it's great being a life-changing agent!

A Well-Focused Goal

Peter also admonishes us, "Set your hope fully on the grace to be given you when Jesus Christ is revealed" (1:13). There is a coming day when Christ will return, and at His return He will establish His eternal kingdom. This is the orientation of the believer. It is all too easy for us to be more oriented to now than to then, to here than to there, to ourselves than to Him. The result is a secularized life with quasi-Christian connotations. If my orientation is toward Him, and to then and there, I will be concerned to do and to be that which pleases Him and which will count in eternity.

A good rule of thumb when you're looking at your lifestyle is to ask yourself questions, such as, "How would this particular relationship play there?" Or "How would this particular habit play then?" "How would this particular activity look before Him?" It is a well-established fact that if you aim at nothing, you'll probably hit it. But there need be no fear of a wasted life or a meaningless existence if the goal of life is to be pleasing to the Lord at His return and in view of His kingdom, and to live each day in the light of these facts. It produces holiness too!

We Who Are Redeemed Accept Our Responsibilities

Making Decisions

When God made human beings, He invested them with decision-making capabilities. He was not being capricious when He told them they could enjoy everything in the garden that was lovely—except the forbidden fruit. His intention was not to create an environment in which forbidden fruit would prove to be sweeter. Rather, He was giving human beings the opportunity to discover one of the major distinctives of their humanity. They had the ability to make informed decisions; they had been given the dignity status of decision-makers. This ability and dignified status have never been withdrawn, even though the ability is abused and our decisions could not always be characterized as dignified.

There is much emphasis in modern society about human beings being the unfortunate victims of forces outside themselves. While true to a certain extent, this becomes invalid when it leads to the conclusion that the ability to choose and the accountability of choices made has been cancelled. The reasons given for choices being made may well be correct; but denial of the responsibility of the one choosing is not only incorrect but is positively demeaning.

Much of the confusion on this point has slipped insidiously into Christian thinking, with the result that lifestyles which are far from holy are regarded as unexceptional, and the offending behavior is characterized as unavoidable. If that is true, then the commands of Scripture summed up in "Be holy because I am holy" are a joke. But God isn't laughing.

It is necessary for believers, whatever the nature of their predispositions, and whatever the diagnosis of those predispositions, to recognize that if they are engaging in behaviors incompatible with a holy lifestyle, they can and they must make the necessary decisions to put matters right.

Establishing Necessary Disciplines

Unless alcoholics make a decision to stop drinking, they won't stop. But the decision is not enough. They have to build into their lives simple but basic disciplines, like refusing to take a job as a barman, declining invitations to a boozy party, empty-ing their liquor cabinet and pouring the booze down the sink, and joining an accountability group.

Pornography addicts may come to a conclusion that they have succumbed to addictive behavior that is wrong as well as damaging, and it must therefore stop. But the decision will not be sufficient in itself. Discipline needs to be built in. They will need to cancel magazine subscriptions, unhook some cable channels, sell their video machine, install blockers in their com-puters, perhaps travel to and from work by a different route to avoid tempting bookstores or movie houses, and in all probabil-ity get professional help.

These are extreme illustrations, but they serve to make the point which needs to be applied in all manner of situations. And the point is that if you decide a certain behavior is in-compatible with holiness, then you must build disciplines into your life which will serve to assist in maintaining the decision made.

Encouraging Right Desires

Computer people tell us, "Garbage in, garbage out." Any preacher will tell you the same thing. If the input into a life is contrary to holiness, the output will not be a holy lifestyle. We have already seen that we need to consider the question, "What do we need to give up?" But there is another balancing question: "What do we need to start up?"

We will look into this more thoroughly in the following chapters, but for now let me remind you that believers are in-dwelt by the Holy Spirit, the Spirit of holiness, as Paul calls Him (Rom. 1:4). He is concerned to prompt us to proper desires and to "nerve our faint endeavor" in the direction of holiness. He imparts noble aspirations and stimulates higher longings; He raises our sights and leads us to aim higher.

We therefore need to nourish and nurture the life of the Spirit. If we don't, it will be a case of "Garbage in, garbage out." But if we do, it will be a matter of "Fruitful thinking in, fruit of the Spirit out."

PRAYER

We bow before Your holiness, dear heavenly Father, and thank You that though we in our sinfulness were estranged from Your presence, You have graciously taken the initiative and sent Christ to be our Redeemer, to buy us back, so that we might become Your people.

We recognize that You in Your holiness have called us to Yourself and to live a holy life. We recognize the struggles that this entails, but we thank You for what Scripture tells us. It tells us that we can order our minds. It tells us that we can build in discipline. It tells us that we can get our goals and objectives right. It tells us that the Spirit of the living God can so work in our hearts that He will give us new aspirations and longings, new abilities and new powers, and begin to produce the fruit of holiness in us.

The more we think about these things and the more we talk about them, we recognize how inadequate our lives are. So we call upon You for mercy, and we ask You graciously to continue Your work in us and through us. Hear our prayers, for we present them in the name of our Lord Jesus—our Lord, our Savior and our Redeemer. Amen.

A Personal Note from Jill

Holiness, I have noticed, doesn't just "happen" without our very definite cooperation. That is because it involves discipline, and discipline involves decisions that God has determined that "I" not "He" will make. He wants me to take responsibility for my own choices and their consequences. But how does this work out in real life?

I remember wondering that one day as I opened my mail. I was an excited freshman at an education college in Cambridge, England. I discovered there was plenty to do with my spare time—all sorts of clubs and societies, sports, culture and debates, and, of course, endless social opportunities. It was like another world—a wonderful, sophisticated student supermarket. It was as if my wonderful parents had given me a blank check and a cart, and set me off down the laden aisles with the heady realization I had the wherewithal to choose what I would.

Shortly after arriving there, however, I became a Christian. Now I faced exactly the same choices as before, but the importance of my choices was eternal. Before my conversion it had been a struggle to choose the right things to do because of my "good" family background that influenced me. Now I didn't have a mere struggle—I had a war on my hands!

Part of the added pressure was the activity of Satan. When you belong to him, he doesn't bother you too much. But when you become a Christian, his fury knows no bounds. He magnifies the world's attractions to tempt you to be unfaithful, plays on the flesh or the "old" part of you and occasionally appears himself as an angel of light, but always with devilish motives in mind.

I had enjoyed my round of parties before I was converted; now I took another look at the invitation lying in my hands. It was creatively written with suggestive overtones that tantalized the imagination. It was going to be a wild one. I knew that the Bible did not say, "Don't go to a party," but I also knew it demanded a "different" lifestyle of me—a lifestyle that would not be compatible with the goings-on at this particular party.

But I wanted to go! I had joined the famous Cambridge dramatic society, The Footlights, and while I had a very lowly part in it all, I was captivated by the worldly-wise, handsome director and the super-intelligent, zany people who made up the cast of characters. This was their party. They had not needed to invite me, but they had. What's more, this would be the very first party invitation I had ever turned down!

A disciple asks his master what to do in such circumstances. I turned to my Bible and the reading for the day. When Bible reading is a daily discipline, God has a chance to meet you in the pages of His Book. And that is just what He did for me. "Remove your foot from evil," I read. Well, that seemed a bit dramatic, I thought. After all, my friends weren't really "evil," just out for a good time. I read on, chasing the references from that particular verse around the Scriptures. They led me to "lead us not into temptation, but deliver us from evil." Then I realized that if I deliberately walked into temptation, I could not expect God to deliver me from evil. I knew myself well enough not to trust my willpower in that particular "nicely evil" party! And so I penned my regrets to the invitation.

I realized that another day, at another time, it might well be God's will to accept such an invitation in order to bring light into a dark place. But I knew I wasn't strong enough, ready enough or willing enough to do that—not a wise enough a believer to be that light just yet.

A lifestyle has to be learned and then practiced, and part of that comes with being honest enough with yourself to know your particular weak spots and wait until God has dealt with them before you put your testimony at risk. Yes, the Bible does say, "Live such good lives among the pagans," and some might argue, "That's why you have to go to the party." But I was able to honestly look at my innermost motivation and know at that time that I did not want to go to be light, but rather to enjoy the darkness. Holiness requires honesty with God, yourself and other people.

Some days later a friend who had attended the said event stopped and asked me, "Why didn't you come?"

"Was it as wild as it sounded?" I asked.

"Sure," she replied. "So why didn't you come?"

"I couldn't trust myself to come," I answered. She looked at me quite stunned!

"What do you mean?" she asked in amazement. So I told her about Jesus whom I had just come to know, and what differences in my behavior I believed were required of me now. I didn't win her to Christ, but a seed was sown that someone else would reap one day.

CHAPTER QUESTIONS

1. We are God's people because He made us and bought us. The discipline of holiness requires honesty and willingness to be obedient and also a dose of sheer common sense! We are twice His. Do you feel a sense of security, of belonging? Do you have an attitude of gratitude when you think of this? Try to honestly assess your motivation for living a holy life. Is it:

   a. Fear?

    b. Habit?

    c. Peer pressure?

    d. Gratitude to God?

    e. Modeling after a Christian you admire?

    f. A desire to please someone?

Gratitude motivates us to holiness consistently. Make a list of all the spiritual things about your salvation for which you are grateful to God. Then spend a few moments praising Him for them.

2. Reread the illustration about being in the army (it is after the subhead, "He Who Has Provided Redemption Has Outlined His Requirements"). Have you ever "worn the uniform of the enemy"? Has there been a time when you committed spiritual treason? Think about an incident when this happened. Ask God to forgive and cleanse you.

3. Which of these three aspects do you need to work on most?

    a. A well-ordered mind (Rom. 12:1–2)

    b. A well-disciplined lifestyle (Phil. 1:27)

    c. A well-focused goal (3:14)

Read the verse beside the one aspect you need to work on, and respond to it in prayer.

4. Read Titus 2:1–10 for some practical instructions about holiness. What do you learn from this text

    a. about God?

    b. about Christians?

    c. about non-Christians?

    d. about yourself?

5. Pray about these practical instructions concerning a holy lifestyle.

5

ঙ

THE SPIRIT OF HOLINESS

So I say, live by the Spirit, and you will not gratify the desires of the sinful nature. For the sinful nature desires what is contrary to the Spirit, and the Spirit what is contrary to the sinful nature. They are in conflict with each other, so that you do not do what you want. But if you are led by the Spirit, you are not under law. . . . Those who belong to Christ Jesus have crucified the sinful nature with its passions and desires. Since we live by the Spirit, let us keep in step with the Spirit. (GAL. 5:16–18, 24–25)

As we have seen, God calls us to live a holy lifestyle. But if you are like me, you have no doubt discovered that it is one thing to have holy aspirations and another to succeed in living a holy life. In my younger days this anomaly caused me considerable heartache and confusion until I discovered the teaching of the apostle Paul on the subject. To my intense delight I read that he too had struggled at this point—proving once again that "misery loves company"!

The quotation from Paul's letter to the Galatians is key to understanding what he taught the Galatian believers, for he gave them (and us) both a realistic appraisal of what we could call "the holiness tension" (between aspiration and performance) and God's provision for resolving it. In short, he reminds us of the age-old, heartwarming principle that "God never calls without equipping." And that equipping—if we may so call it—is found in a relationship with the Holy Spirit, or as He is sometimes called, the Spirit of holiness (Rom. 1:4).

While the apostle Paul was in Galatia, he had emphasized the subject of Christian freedom, and he returned to that theme in his epistle as he reminded the Galatians, "It is for freedom that Christ has set us free" (5:1) and "You, my brothers, were called to be free" (5:13).

Mention "freedom" in most quarters and people's ears will prick up! There is something exciting and appealing about freedom, whether we live in countries ruled by oppressive regimes or we simply chafe at rules and regulations that are impediments to the fulfillment of our reckless desires.

But what did Paul mean by freedom? He was particularly addressing his Jewish readers. They had taken the law of Moses very seriously, and rightly so. In fact, they had exhibited such a commendable desire to live rightly by the law that they had asked for—and received—specific clarifications, interpretations and practical instructions so that they could avoid breaking the law inadvertently. So instead of broad generalities like "Love the Lord your God with all your heart and soul and strength," and "Love your neighbor as yourself," they now had hundreds of rules and regulations that defined what loving God looked like and who the neighbors they were to love were and were not!

All these amplifications they were admonished to observe. But in the multitude of instructions, there were abundant opportunities for failure, and understandably, that is precisely what they were doing. As a result, they were living in bondage to frustrating feelings of inadequacy (if they admitted failure) or in bondage to hypocrisy (if they faked it)! Bondage on every hand!

When Paul arrived on the scene, he said, "Look, nobody is ever justified by keeping the law. There never was a human being who fulfilled the letter and the spirit of the Ten Commandments, and no one is ever going to get to heaven because they kept them in their entirety. And partial occasional adherence to them won't do" (see Gal. 3:10). That was the bad news, and the people were, no doubt, deeply chagrined to hear it.

But then Paul gave them the good news: "You and your own efforts cannot make your sinfulness—failures, shortcomings—acceptable to God's holiness, but God has sent His Son to die on the cross so that your sins might be forgiven. You can therefore be made acceptable to a Holy God, not on the basis of keeping the law, but on the basis of the cross of Christ and His free forgiveness made available to you." Those who believed his message found it tremendously liberating, and therefore, they set out in a new direction, potentially free from the old way of life. Freedom!

Spiritual Conflict

However, after Paul left Galatia other teachers followed him and endeavored to dismantle his message and ministry. They said, "Now listen, what Paul is teaching you is all right as far as it goes, but it has a fatal flaw in it. He says that your keeping of the law will not lead to a right relationship with God—only faith that accepts His grace demonstrated in Christ's death and resurrection will do that for you. But that is not enough. In addition to faith and grace, you need to keep the works of the law—the old rules and regulations particularly those regarding circumcision and food."

What this meant to the new believers is plain to see. Paul preached a message that brought them "freedom" (from all these laws), and the teachers who had followed him tried to reinstate the laws leading to "bondage." No wonder the Galatian believers were confused—some to the point of trying to hold on to Paul's gospel and the "gospel" of his critics at the same time. Paul wrote his letter to the Galatians to counter these contrary teachings and to encourage the new believers in their experience of Christian liberty, the pathway to holiness of life.

We may wonder how this first-century problem can possibly say anything of relevance to the twenty-first century. I doubt if most of us know of anyone who is going around churches telling young believers that they need to be circumcised and keep the ancient food laws if they want to be reconciled to God! Furthermore, we may ask, What does this have to do with the issue raised at the beginning of this chapter—namely the issue of the call to holy living being beyond our natural capabilities? Patience friends—we're getting there!

It is true that the modern situation differs dramatically from the one Paul encountered—in specifics but not in principle, as we shall see. Today we don't worry about circumcision, etc., but there are situations in which earnest believers, out of a fear that we may take our faith too lightly, insist on rules laying out in detail what constitutes legitimate living that leads to holiness. So for instance, strict rules about skirt length, hair length and make-up, as well as restrictions on what to drink (but not how much to eat) and on watching movies (but not DVDs), etc. are not uncommon in some circles.

We call this—not entirely accurately—"legalism." It can be a modern-day bondage, for it suggests that holiness is solely the product of human effort; it's a bondage that imposes rules on believers on issues where the Scripture remains silent or at least less than definitive.

But wait a moment, say the believers who, from their point of view, believe that moral and spiritual standards tend to slip if not carefully safeguarded. (From my vantage point as an eighty-year-old believer, I think many standards have indeed slipped in my lifetime. But that's what you can expect from an old curmudgeon!) If we just tell people they are "free," they say, the old adage "give them an inch and they'll take a mile" takes over. And they have a point!

Actually, Paul seems to have confronted a similar situation. He was not only dealing with legalism. He apparently had proponents of "license" on his hands as well. Note what he wrote to the Galatians: "You, my brothers, were called to be free. But do not use your freedom to indulge the sinful nature" (Gal. 5:13).

It is interesting to surmise what exactly Paul was referring to in this exhortation. We do know that many of the people Paul ministered to had been deeply influenced by Greek philosophy. It was commonly believed that "matter" (including the human body) was sinful and only spirit was good. Accordingly, for many of them, what you did with and in your body was of no consequence because the body was bound for destruction anyway. That opened the door to a purely sensual, materialistic, ill-disciplined, carefree life given over to all manner of licentious behavior. Oscar Wilde with his love of "excess" would have been perfectly at home in their midst.

Perhaps these were the people Paul had in mind when he warned against using Christian freedom as a mandate to "indulge the sinful nature." He was coping with the opposite extremes of legalism and licentiousness at the same time! Like the cavalrymen involved in "The Charge of the Light Brigade," who faced "Cannons to right of them, cannons to the left of them," Paul and his gospel were being shot at from both sides—legalism to the right of them, license to the left of them!

Over the years preachers of holiness have not been shot at, but their message has frequently been opposed, both by those who see holiness as the product of rules and regulations and those who see holiness as an unwarranted and unwelcome imposition on their gospel freedom! Or to put it another way, legalism and licentiousness have this in common: both are enemies of holiness, and neither will ever produce it! But there's more.

Two Problems, One Root Cause

Paul appears to say that there is one root cause of both legalistic and licentious behavior. This, at first, seems hard to believe, but note exactly what he wrote to the Galatians: "Did you receive the Spirit by observing the law, or by believing what you heard? Are you so foolish? After beginning with the Spirit, are you now trying to attain your goal by human effort? [lit., are you seeking to be perfected by the flesh?]" (3:2–3).

Who is Paul addressing? He's speaking to those who received the Spirit through the hearing of faith, but who were now seeking spiritual growth (holiness) through the rules and regulations of the law! Legalists. And what does he say about them? That their problem is something he calls "the flesh." Note that.

Now look again at the verse we noted earlier: "Do not use your freedom to indulge the sinful nature [lit., the flesh]" (5:13). Who is he addressing here? He is speaking to those who are the opposite of legalists; those committed to licentious living! But their problem is also "the flesh"! Surprisingly, Paul states that "flesh" is the root problem for those who prefer a life of careless indulgence to a life of holiness and also the root problem for those whose careful approach to a holy life is paved with rules and regulations.

This is where we come in. As we noted at the beginning of the chapter, the key to developing a holy life is the relationship we enjoy with the Holy Spirit. But—and this is an important "but"—Paul wrote that "the sinful nature (the flesh) desires what is contrary to the Spirit and the Spirit what is contrary to the sinful nature" (5:17). That means we not only have to nurture a relationship with the Holy Spirit, but we also need to be fully aware of "the flesh" and know how to deal with its contrary activities and its negative impact on our lives.

"The sinful nature" and "the flesh" are two translations of the same Greek word—*sarx*, a word that appears in a variety of ways in the Scriptures. Sometimes it refers literally to flesh—part of the physical body. Other times it can mean people, as in "flesh and blood"; in some instances it refers to humanity in general. In Paul's writings, however, it frequently takes on a moral dimension, in which case it refers to the *fallenness* of humanity. This can be seen clearly in such statements as "I know that nothing good lives in me, that is in my sinful nature [*sarx*]" (Rom. 7:18) or "Those controlled by the sinful nature [*sarx*] cannot please God" (8:8).

G.K. Chesterton said that people don't agree on very much, but they're all agreed that there's something wrong with humanity. He firmly believed that the thing wrong with humanity is deep down inside us. Paul called it "the flesh." And he insisted that the flesh is the unrelenting opponent of the Spirit of holiness.

It is this understanding that has led many scholars to suggest that "flesh" means a human being devoid of the Holy Spirit—humanity in its fallen natural state. The flesh is human beings in their natural condition in action as opposed to human beings in tune with the supernatural in action. The flesh is independence run riot, when we were created to be dependent agents of the Holy Spirit at work.

The sinful nature loves to do things its own way. In some people it has a bias to self-effort, in others a bias to self-indulgence. But always it features the self. So self-effort finds in religion an ideal environment in which to display its innate powers of self-reliance rather than humble dependence and self-improvement rather than divine transformation. Then if the flesh can impose its methods of self-improvement on its neighbors and insist on its own proofs of self-reliance for others, legalism triumphs, the flesh rules and the Spirit is declared redundant.

Freedom and Flesh

The flesh also manifests itself in self-indulgence. It wants to be "free to be me." It wants to be free to do whatever it wants to do, and what it wants to do is not pretty. Paul had some powerful things to say about this and predicated them with the trenchant observation that "The acts of the sinful nature are obvious" (5:19). It ought to be as obvious to us as it was to Paul that much of what passes for freedom today is actually the flesh at work. In case there is any confusion on this point, let's look at the rest of that verse: "The acts of the sinful nature are obvious . . . [including] sexual immorality, impurity and debauchery."

When I was preaching this material in my home church, somebody told a friend, "Let me know when he finishes this series, and I'll come back." Someone else sent word to me: "Your views on sexuality are prehistoric." Unfortunately, I was not able to talk to the person in question because he communicated anonymously. But that person had a very keen insight—my views on sexuality *are* prehistoric!

Since history is man's record of events, you can't have history until you have man. Therefore, anything which is prehistoric is really pre-man-as-historian. I freely admit and enthusiastically affirm that my views on sexuality not only predate man-as-historian, but they predate man. They originate in the heart of God—they are a fundamental part of the created order. We move away from them at our peril.

In the same way that God ordained physical laws for the physical universe, He instituted societal laws for the social arena. One of those laws is that sexuality is a gift of God to be enjoyed in the context of faithful, monogamous, heterosexual marriage. With all the talk of sexual revolution and freedom of expression and individual rights, the church should be saying loudly and clearly, "Whatever terms you wish to employ to describe the modern revamping of traditional sexual morality, please be aware that what you are doing is perfectly "obvious" to those with eyes to see. It's the flesh! It's the sinful nature! It's fallen humanity expressing its independence of God!"

Bishop William Frey put it this way:

> Many of us believe that the sexual revolution has run its course, leaving in its wake thousands of broken marriages, a sharp rise in teenage pregnancies, millions of convenience-motivated abortions, a multibillion dollar pornography industry, and a mushrooming AIDS epidemic. What could be better news than the proclamation that there is a better way?[7]

Amen to the Episcopal bishop. We need to recognize that sexual immorality is an obvious manifestation of the sinful nature insisting on self-indulgence in the area of sexuality.

Paul's list continued with other obvious manifestations of the flesh, this time in the area of religion. He listed "idolatry and witchcraft." Idolatry is the worship of that which is created in the place of worship of the Creator. It's the ultimate insult! And contrary to conventional wisdom, it is not limited to heathen and pagan societies, but is also part of the prevailing attitude of the Western industrialized democracies. A very solid case could be made for rampant idolatry being the religion of the materialistic West. If we are honest, we need to admit that it is easier to worship the blessing than the blesser. And who of us would be able to say, "I instinctively find myself infinitely more interested in the Creator than my love of what He has created"? The truth of the matter is that we have a sinful nature which very often leads us to idolatry.

Paul also talked about witchcraft, which is an acknowledgment of the forces of darkness to the extent that they become more important than the "Father of the heavenly lights." Even a cursory survey of popular novels, TV shows, comic books and movies will show the proliferation of this type of attraction. It is also obvious where it stems from!

The sinful nature is also at work in personal relationships. Listed specifically are "hatred, discord, jealousy, fits of rage, selfish ambition, dissension, factions and envy." Self-indulgence can take over relationships and manifest itself in a thousand different ways. And who of us would say that we have been totally free all our lives from these sordid and sad manifestations of sarx? But how often do we call them what they really are? How much more likely we are to ignore or excuse, rationalize or psychologize what God exposes as the sinful nature. Paul's list concludes with "drunkenness, orgies and the like," which are further demonstrations of self-indulgence in uncontrolled excessive behavior. It's all so obvious!

God Sent His Spirit

The sinful nature is not eradicated when we come to faith, but we do receive the Holy Spirit. So while the believer has to acknowledge the ongoing presence of the flesh, there must also be a recognition of the presence of the Holy Spirit. Paul explained in Galatians 3:14 that God redeemed us "so that by faith we might receive the promise of the Spirit." Then he added that in the same way that "God sent His Son" (4:4) to die for us, He "sent the Spirit of His Son into our hearts" (4:6). We don't have one without the other. He sent His Son to die for us and the Spirit of His Son to live in us. If Christ had died for us but God had not sent His Spirit, it would be a case of our being forgiven for sinning, but at the same time being left totally unable to do anything but to go on sinning. But He gave the Son to die for us, and He sent the Spirit of His Son to live in us to give us the power to live in newness of life. The key, therefore, to holiness of life is to be found in the Spirit of holiness who comes into our fallenness both to counteract its nefarious influence and to produce in us that which glorifies God.

Paul characterized this life as "the fruit of the Spirit," which he described as "love, joy, peace, patience, kindness, goodness, faithfulness, gentleness and self-control" (5:22–23). Or in a word, holiness! The fruit of the Spirit is a description of holiness in action, and its evidence is as obvious as the outworking of the flesh; but the two are as different as an orchard and a slum.

So why do we have to cope with license and legalism? Because the sinful nature was not eradicated when we came to faith. What hope is there for us? Our hope is in the sending of the Spirit of God, the Spirit of holiness, into our lives. However, we have to accept the fact that the flesh and the Spirit are in total opposition to each other. That is why, in a very real sense, the soul of the believer is a battlefield.

Do you remember the story of Rebecca, Isaac's wife? Rebecca was having a hard time with her pregnancy, and so she prayed, understandably, "Why is this happening to me?" (Gen. 25:22). This was not simple morning sickness; she felt as if a war was going on inside her—which is exactly what was happening. The Lord explained that she was pregnant with twins. Two boys who already detested each other were pushing and shoving inside her womb. They were born feuding, and they spent much of their lives plotting and conniving. All believers who are earnest about spiritual life and concerned about holiness recognize similar internal struggles.

Paul, in a great autobiographical statement, put it this way: "What I want to do I do not do, but what I hate I do" (Rom. 7:15). He admitted that he had noble aspirations which fell flat on their face. He made great decisions to change that didn't work. Eventually he said, "What a wretched man I am!" (7:24). He was graphically describing his internal conflict. We need to follow Paul's example and confront the fact that holiness is a struggle and that it is so easy to swerve into legalism or slide into license.

Living by the Spirit

I would not be at all surprised if, at this point, you are thinking that the battle is too much, that a holy life is an unattainable dream and that you will just settle for as acceptable a lifestyle as you can reasonably manage. The subtle danger of that resigned approach is that it is a surrender to sarx, for it discounts the Holy Spirit and settles for the natural at the expense of the supernatural. That won't do! Instead of resigning ourselves to "doing the best we can," God calls us to focus on His Spirit. Paul explained it in straightforward terms, "Those who belong to Christ Jesus have crucified the sinful nature with its passions and desires. Since we live by the Spirit, let us keep in step with the Spirit" (Gal. 5:24–25). Then he added, "A man reaps what he sows" (6:7). These verses contain four basic spiritual considerations that we need to understand and apply.

Believers "Belong to Christ Jesus"

We need to understand that Christ *owns* us. Why? First, because we were created; second, because God gave us to Christ (John 17:24); and third, because Christ redeemed us and bought us for Himself. We've addressed these topics in previous chapters. But we need to apply it personally and ask ourselves, "Do I regard myself as belonging to *Him*, or do I regard myself as belonging to *me*? Whose rights am I most interested in, mine or His?"

When you buy a house, you pay your money and the house becomes your property. Then there comes a point at which you take possession. What would you think if you got your bunch of keys, went to your new house and found all the doors locked, and none of your keys would open them? The house would be your property, but for all practical purposes you would be denied possession because the previous owner who had traded his rights had actually kept control.

Apply the analogy in terms of the spiritual life. I invite Christ by His Spirit to become Savior and Lord and to indwell my life. I become His property. I belong to Him. The problem, however, is that sometimes I give Him the bunch of keys but change the locks on a number of the doors. I'm going to keep those areas to myself because I want to indulge the flesh in one way or another. It may be in the area of my worship of created things rather than the Creator. It may be in the area of my sexuality. It may be in the area of my interpersonal relationships where I'm not going to forgive, and I'm not willing to be reconciled. If I belong to Christ, I am His property, and I must change the locks and surrender the keys.

Believers "Have Crucified the Sinful Nature"

This statement does not mean that the sinful nature is dead. It is painfully obvious that it isn't! What then does it mean? Notice first that Paul said "those who belong to Christ Jesus have crucified the sinful nature." Apparently he was conveying the fact that at the time we transferred ownership of our lives to Christ by acknowledging Him as Lord and Savior, another transaction was also completed: the sinful nature was crucified.

Look at it this way. Paul said, "May I never boast except in the cross" (Gal. 6:14). That is an appropriate attitude for someone who recognizes the holiness of God and the sinfulness of man, and knows that sinful man can never enter into the presence of a holy God except by the cross of Christ. Accordingly, he boasts in the cross. Those who boast in the cross know that they cannot boast in it and also continue to live in the things that made the cross necessary—that's obvious! Those who acknowledge the simple fact that it was necessary for Christ to die for them know that they do not have the freedom to live in those things which made His death a necessity. They accept that they are no longer free to live in what He chose to die for.

So when we came to Christ, we also came to the cross, and as our sin, guilt and condemnation were dealt with there (and we boast about that!), so also our unregenerate, natural self that was responsible for all the sin and guilt was also dealt with there. Those things were put on the cross; we turned from them and said, "Those things have no further claim on my life. The old life and the old way of doing things are no longer my way of living." In this sense, we have "crucified the sinful nature."

In some ways it's similar to what happened on my wedding day. When I came to Jill as husband, at that moment I walked away from singleness. That does not mean I have automatically always behaved like a husband and never resembled a single man. In fact, that reminds me of a story.

After ten years of traveling extensively all over the world on my own, I switched gears; my family and I moved into a pastoral role in an American church. At the end of the service the first Sunday night I preached there, I did what I always did when I was traveling—I went home. But I absent-mindedly left without my wife and children—hardly the behavior of a married man!

Despite such occasional memory lapses, I know I am a married man, and I act accordingly. I live in the recognition that I have a wife and family. In a sense I have "crucified" the single life; it no longer has a claim on me.

Believers "Live by the Spirit"

Having recognized that the spiritual life is not produced by self-effort or self-indulgence, but is the result of a relationship with the Spirit of holiness, we see that the nurturing and nourishing of the Spirit is of paramount importance. Therefore, our focus must move from the flesh to the Spirit, who will give us new desires, lead us in new directions and introduce new distinctives.

It is probably true to say that some believers embark on a spiritual journey with little or no comprehension of the role of the Spirit of holiness. As a result, they may slip into a careless and indifferent attitude that becomes more or less satisfied with a lifestyle that differs very little from that of an unbeliever except for their attendance, however spasmodic, at a place of worship. Or they may set about following the example of believers who show them the ropes, explain what is acceptable and what isn't, and allow themselves to be introduced to a pattern of living which owes more to the specific requirements and expectations of Christian subculture than a relationship with the Spirit of holiness.

Paul's instruction is as clear as it is logical. "Since we live by the Spirit, let us keep in step with the Spirit." From my experience as a member of the Royal Marines' ceremonial drill squad, I can testify to the great sense of exhilaration, rhythm and purpose that comes from marching in step. And, conversely, the great sense of disjointedness and embarrassment that comes when the rhythm is lost. To keep in step with the Spirit is to know a deep sense of well-being and purpose. To be out of step is to be out of touch and out of sorts.

Believers "Reap What they Sow"

A lot of people don't even know that this old adage comes from the Bible. We all know that if we plant turnips we don't get tulips. We plant turnips and grow turnips. We plant tulips and grow tulips. We should also recognize that if we sow to the flesh we'll produce destruction, and if we sow to the Spirit we'll produce life—that's the age-old principle. So we need to ask ourselves these questions:

- Do I honestly believe that I belong to Christ?

- Do I boast in the cross and show it in the way that I have crucified that old life?

- Do I believe that I no longer have the freedom to live in the things it was necessary for Him to die for?

- Do I now live in the Spirit, believing that in His power alone I will find new desires, directions and distinctives?

- Do I recognize that if I insist on sowing to the flesh by nurturing and encouraging, feeding and pampering it, I will produce destruction in my life and other people's lives, but if I live after the Spirit, the result will be life?

PRAYER

We come quietly before You, dear Lord, and recognize that we have heard Your word—a searching, powerful, challenging and encouraging word. In the quietness of our hearts, we want to reaffirm the fact that we belong to You, and we are happy to give You the keys that fit the locks. Lord, we freely admit that we have tended to nurture and nourish the sinful nature, and we have reaped what we've sowed.

We would like to acknowledge the Spirit within us, and to ask Him to plow into that old sinful nature and begin to produce in us that which will glorify You and produce a life of holiness. Lord, hear our prayer, in Christ's name. Amen.

A Personal Note from Jill

There is nowhere that the battle between the flesh and the Spirit rages with more force in my life than in the area of my devotional disciplines. I, like Peter, James and John in the Garden of Gethsemane, have to be reawakened far too often by the Lord and told to watch and pray lest I enter into temptation!

As soon as the alarm goes off in the morning, the flesh reaches out a determined finger and shuts it off, so the rest of me can sink into unconsciousness again. The flesh has won! It seems such an easy thing to do—to get up one half-hour earlier than planned in order to meet with God. But the devil knows how important it is and will bring all his forces to bear on the one who determines to pray and study God's Word. As the saying goes, "The devil trembles when he sees the weakest saint upon his knees."

The devil will try and busy us with doing for God instead of being with God. A focus on God things—instead of God Himself—is a common way he tempts the old nature in us. The self-nature likes to do God's business, but finds it goes against his self-righteous nature to simply be in God's holy presence and do personal business.

The world offers good substitutes too, like an exercise program before devotions. The Spirit meanwhile is quietly insisting you have your devotions first and then exercise!

As soon as I began my Christian walk, I became aware of this daily battle within. I talked to many people about it, trying to figure out how I could best make sure I did what the Spirit wanted me to do. In the end I came to an unavoidable conclusion: there was no one in the whole wide world but me who could say no to the flesh and yes to the Spirit. People could talk to me till they were blue in the face. I could have a well-thought-out plan like the one I describe in Chapter 2. I could read books and listen to tapes on the subject. But in the end it came down to my will or won't!

I thought about the sheep in Psalm 23 and realized the shepherd did not move their little mouths up and down to make them chew on grass. He provided the grass, but they had to settle down and digest it! It would be so much easier if we didn't have a choice, yet God gives us a will to exercise. And who would want to be a puppet on a string rather than a human being with the chance to choose?

The problem I have is that this is a daily choice. I have learned the old nature in me will feel as sleepy tomorrow as it did yesterday! For the rest of my life, I will have to take my will in hand and let the alarm do its work—get up and get on with it. Yesterday's victory over the flesh will not "dribble" over into today.

One thing I try to do day by day that really helps me exercise my will rightly is to remember the time I sang the beautiful hymn "Take My Life" right from my heart. Particularly the verse that says, "Take my will and make it Thine, it shall be no longer mine." I remember making a promise that my will was His forever. Since then, day by day I need to ratify that original commitment on a moment by moment basis. This way I will "keep in step with the Spirit" instead of running ahead of Him or tripping over my own fleshly feet!

Chapter Questions

1. Did you have "religious rules" as a child—either ones taught to you or ones you made up yourself? Try writing down your own "Ten Commandments" from childhood (such as,

"Thou shalt get good grades" or "It's OK to lie if no one gets hurt").

2. Paul says, "The acts of the sinful nature are obvious." Which of these acts seem the most rampant in your world?

    a. sexual immorality

    b. idolatry

    c. witchcraft

    d. destruction of relationships

3. By contrast, in Galatians 5:22–23 Paul speaks of the acts of the Spirit in our lives producing obvious blessing. These acts are love, joy, peace, patience, kindness, goodness, faithfulness, gentleness and self-control.

    a. All these are aspects of holiness. Circle the aspects of holiness you see in some measure in your own life. Pray about those not circled.

    b. In this chapter the comment is made, "To be 'out of touch' is to be 'out of sorts.'" Is this your experience? Can you pinpoint the place where you lost touch? Pray about it.

4. Read Romans 7:14–25.

    a. In verse 14 Paul calls himself unspiritual. What does that say to you?

    b. Is there anything good in our sinful nature (see 7:18)? Is this your experience?

    c. What do you "keep on doing" (7:19) that you would like to stop?

    d. How is this struggle described (see 7:22)?

e.   Who can make the difference (see 7:25)?

5. Read Romans 8:1–17. Make a list of verses—and then write them out—that answer your personal heart need concerning the battle inside you. Pray about them.

6

❧

OFFER YOUR BODIES AS HOLY

Therefore, I urge you, brothers, in view of God's mercy, to offer your bodies as living sacrifices, holy and pleasing to God—this is your spiritual act of worship. Do not conform any longer to the pattern of this world, but be transformed by the renewing of your mind. Then you will be able to test and approve what God's will is—His good, pleasing, and perfect will. (ROM. 12:1–2)

As we have seen, the word holiness has as its basic meaning "separation." Unfortunately, when some people hear "separation," they think "isolation." They believe that committing to a life of holiness will isolate them from reality, put them out of touch with the mainstream and relegate them to the sidelines, there to watch the rest of the world go by. A few people find this very appealing (and promptly disappear into a monastery), but the vast majority find it desperately unattractive and say, "Forget it."

John White described his own reactions when he thought of holiness. He said the immediate associations in his mind were "thinness, hollow-eyed gauntness, beards, sandals, long robes, stone cells, no sex, no jokes, hair shirts, frequent cold baths, fasting, hours of prayer, wild rocky deserts, getting up at 4 a.m., clean fingernails, stained glass and self-humiliation."[8]

However, while these perceptions are certainly overdone, we must recognize that to be "separated" will often require being separated from some aspects of contemporary life and culturally acceptable behaviors. But the predominant biblical emphasis is more toward what we are separated for. What this means we shall now explore.

Sacrificial Lifestyle

The book of Romans is rightly revered as perhaps the greatest definitive statement of the Christian faith. For the first eleven intense, carefully reasoned chapters of the epistle, Paul outlined the gospel and then concluded with a great doxological exclamation of praise: "For from him and through him and to him are all things. To him be the glory forever. Amen" (11:36). It would not have been surprising if Paul had concluded his epistle on that sublime note. But he didn't. Immediately he turned to the practical application of the great theological truths he had outlined. These concluding and essentially practical chapters of Romans contain much that will teach us about what we are separated for, or what practical holiness looks like!

The apostle Paul exhorted the Roman believers, in light of the great good news of the gospel he had carefully explained, to offer themselves as "living sacrifices" that God would regard as holy and pleasing. Now that's a challenge. It is also significant that he said that it was their "bodies" that they were to offer. Clearly he was not advocating they should respond to the gospel by making a literal physical offering of their bodies. Neither was he using an expression that they could conveniently spiritualize. In using the term he was making it clear that he had in mind an essentially down-to-earth and practical response.

Notice particularly the expression "living sacrifices." This sounds suspiciously like an oxymoron, a figure of speech where two mutually contradictory words appear together, like "jumbo shrimp." Surely when we think of sacrifice in the Bible, we think of an animal that winds up dead! How can you have a living sacrifice? If you're living, you're not sacrificed; if you're sacrificed, you're not living!

To understand what Paul meant, turn the expression around. Instead of thinking of living sacrifice, think of sacrificial living, with the accent on lifestyle. He was not talking about isolation or withdrawal from the mainstream. In actual fact, he was calling for a holiness that manifests itself in everyday, mainstream lifestyle.

John White, whose mistaken concepts of holiness we quoted above, went on to say, "While in one sense holiness has to do with the 'wholly other,' yet it must penetrate to the most mundane of our daily activities, so that the division between sacred and secular vanishes entirely from our lives."[9]

There's a very real tendency for us to compartmentalize our lives into the sacred and the secular. Sometimes that's exactly how we want it, because we don't want the one to intrude on the other. But if we begin to think in terms of a lifestyle that is sacrificially separated unto the Lord in the most mundane details of life, we will be much closer to understanding biblical holiness.

But we are getting ahead of ourselves. Let us look carefully at what Paul wrote to the Romans. First of all, notice that God, through the apostle, makes some personal requests. There are three of them:

1. "Offer your bodies as living sacrifices."

2. "Do not conform any longer to the pattern of this world."

3. "Be transformed by the renewing of your mind."

There was a time in my life when I struggled with what I regarded as the demands of God on my life. Then one day I noticed in Romans 12:1 that God wasn't so much "demanding" as "urging" or "encouraging" me to do what He asked. I knew that if I had His kind of authority, I would throw my weight around and demand and command, but He urged and encouraged. That softened my attitude considerably. Notice too that God gave His reasons. We'll touch on these later in the chapter.

God also outlined what will happen if we respond to His requests. When I was growing up, I learned the hard way that I should do what I was told. I was raised in a culture and an age when children were to be seen but not heard. They certainly were not heard asking authority figures, "Why should I do what you say?" One day I tried it and was told frostily by my father, "Because I say so!" That settled it for him but not for me. I suspected he either did not have reasons or they were too fragile and flimsy to bring out into the open!

I noticed, on the other hand, that God not only encouraged action but also volunteered His reasons! And in addition He promised the results in advance. It is certainly easier for us to respond to this than to a more heavy-handed method.

Offering Our Bodies

The request that we offer our bodies is particularly striking when you bear in mind what Paul said about bodies earlier in the epistle. In Romans 6 he pointed out that our bodies can be used as instruments of unrighteousness, and the result is wicked things being done, thought and said. That is something with which we're all familiar.

He went on to say that God did not design our bodies for that purpose, but to be instruments of righteousness. They can actually become the temple of the Holy Spirit. And when He begins to work in our lives, He takes those same members that were instruments of wickedness and uses them as instruments of righteousness. The things we used to do, think and say we no longer do. Instead, we perform helpful acts, think positive thoughts and speak healing words—all with the members of our bodies. The work of God in our lives is to set our bodies free from constantly being the instruments of sin and to liberate them so that they become the instruments of righteousness.

A godly young woman on our church staff recently told the congregation of her previous lifestyle. Many people were shocked to hear what kind of person she had been and the activities in which she had engaged. But she stood before us humbly and radiantly explaining how she was no longer living a life where her body was the medium of wicked activity. As everybody who knows her readily testifies, her whole life is now a channel of blessing. But this had come about because she saw that a body could be used for good or evil—and she had chosen the route of the living sacrifice, the offering of her body to the Lord.

The word offer is very important because it refers to the offering of a sacrifice. It is probably true to say that most people become interested in spiritual life out of a sense of need. They hear that God meets their needs, and so they come to get those needs met. For instance, you'll often find that young children in Christian families hear that one day Jesus will come again, and if He does, Mommy and Daddy are going to go with Him. They get scared that they may be left behind, so they accept Christ out of a great sense of need. I'm sure there are thousands of young people who have come to the Lord in this way. That's perfectly legitimate if it leads to genuine regeneration.

But what about mature adults? Maybe they made a mess of their marriage, and God finally got their attention, and they found the Lord. Or they got into alcohol or drug addiction and faced ruin, but when somebody told them about the Lord, they came to Him. The majority of people, if they were honest, would probably say that they began their spiritual pilgrimage out of a sense of need and a desire for God to meet that need. That's fine, as long as they don't stay there.

Look at it this way. We will experience the saving power of Jesus Christ only in the areas of life where He is Master. To save someone from what binds them, it is necessary for a Savior to master that which binds. The only way that the Allies could function as saviors of Europe in World War II was to master Hitler. Their ability to save was determined by their "lordship." In the same way, as we mature in the Christian faith, we realize that the Lord saves us from that which He masters. It is precisely because He is Lord that He is Savior.

Therefore, it is not enough simply to say, "My Christian experience is that Jesus meets my needs." Somewhere along the line, I must come to the conclusion that the Jesus who meets my needs is the Lord who asks me to commit my life to Him in its entirety, in order that His saving power might be evident in all dimensions of my life. As a teenager in England, I learned a simple chorus which became a life theme:

> Mine are the hands to do Thy work,
> My feet shall run for Thee,
> My lips shall sound the glorious news,
> Lord, here am I, send me.

You may say, "Well, that's what I'm worried about. Where's He going to send me? What is He going to ask me to do?" This kind of trepidation and hesitation is understandable from a purely human point of view because we don't do uncertainty very well. But we need to do better than to limit our perspectives to the human point of view. As we have gained spiritual insight, we should constantly ask ourselves, "Who is our God? Is He the Lord and Savior, is He the Holy One, is He the One who plans for us that which he calls good and perfect and acceptable? If He is, why would we have any reservations about offering our bodies to Him?"

Living Sacrifices

As we've already seen, the offering of our bodies can be understood in terms of a sacrificial lifestyle. That's right and proper, even though we may not be too excited about it. Let's face it, the basis of our blessedness is the cross, and the One who died on the cross calls us to bear our cross. If we are to live as disciples of Jesus Christ, it is a given that there will be elements of sacrifice in the lifestyle to which He calls us.

The extent of sacrifice will vary in every life as determined by the purposes of God. For some people the extent of sacrifice to which He calls will utterly change every dimension of life while for a mercifully smaller number it may call for the sacrifice of life itself. But sacrifice of some kind will undoubtedly be called for.

In his day C.T. Studd was the top cricketer in England. He was absolutely brilliant, the consummate well-rounded man. If cricket is a total mystery to you—as it is to countless people—perhaps baseball may mean more to you. If so, imagine a baseball player who led the league in both hitting and pitching. That was the equivalent of Charlie Studd's performance.

As a young Cambridge student, he became a convinced disciple of Jesus. One day he saw something scribbled on a door that burned into his conscience—just these three words: "Cannibals want missionaries." The anonymous "graffiti artist" may have meant, "Cannibals want medium, rare or well-done missionaries." We don't know what he had in mind, but being British, he probably was addicted to puns! But Charlie Studd interpreted it to mean, "There are some cannibals out there who really want someone to come and tell them how to change their lives."

He had just received half a million dollars from his father. He said he didn't need it so he gave it away; he retired from cricket and took off for China where he spent several years establishing churches. Then he came back home to get recruits, was taken ill, got his recruits, shipped them off, but didn't go back to China himself.

Instead he went to India where he started over again. Years later he came back from India to get more recruits, was taken ill again, and was told that if he left England he would never survive. His doctor described him as a walking museum of tropical diseases.

So he went to Africa and started over for the third time. He didn't have anybody to help him medically, but he read in his Bible that if you anoint with oil and pray, God will heal you. He didn't have any oil so he used kerosene!

Granted, he ran into problems and was labeled by many as "eccentric" and "extremist"—well-earned labels, no doubt! But he offered his body to what he believed God willed for him. The point is that the Lord asks for our willing self-offering to Him for His purposes. Does God have the right to do that? Seeing He asked His Son to die on the cross for us, it would seem to me He has the right to ask the followers of His Son to live sacrificially to the extent of His gracious choosing.

There comes a time when we need to say to ourselves, "I need to think in terms of so committing my life to the Lord that whatever element of sacrifice is necessary in my lifestyle, I will be willing for it." For some married people, that may mean changes in their marriage that they don't want to make. It's quite possible that He's saying to some businesspeople, "There are alterations you need to make as a Christian businessperson." To which the person replies, "But I'll lose the deal!" And Jesus says, "Right! It's called sacrifice."

Some people need to make changes in their associations. "But I love him!" they say. Jesus replies, "I know you do, and you've no business loving him. If you're going to follow the way that I have planned for you, you must recognize that relationship is in neither My interest nor yours. It needs to be offered as a sacrifice." None of this is easy, but neither was the cross.

Paul goes on to say that those who offer their bodies as living sacrifices discover what it means to be holy. We have noted two uses of the word holy. One means "set apart" for someone's use, and the other describes the lifestyle of the called-out person. The former, as we have seen, has been accomplished by the Lord, the latter is a matter of growth and maturity, Holy Spirit activity and our glad cooperation. And both involve sacrifice.

That makes sense. But we need to face our tendency to say, "Lord, how can Jesus be made available to me for my benefit?" We rejoice, and rightly so, in the fact that He is pouring blessings into our lives, but we gag on the thought that He's asking for a life set apart for Him. Of course, if it's going to be set apart to be usable, it's got to be fit to use.

Nonconformity

The second request is, "Don't conform." The third is, "Be

transformed." We need to see these together because the two words are clearly related to each other—we should not be *con*formed but *trans*formed. The root of the Greek word for conform is *schema*, meaning "outward appearance." And the root Greek word for transform is *morphe*, meaning "inner reality." It is relatively easy to keep adjusting the outward appearance— that is conforming. It is an entirely different thing to change the inner reality—that is transforming.

During the Gulf War it took some time to get the military equipment from home base into the desert. Armored divisions were moved from Western Europe to Saudi Arabia, but all the equipment was camouflaged for Western Europe. It was painted different shades of green so that it blended into the plains and forests. If they had put the green equipment in the desert, it would have been too easy for the enemy to spot. Everything had to be recamouflaged. By painting the tanks tan, the equipment was conformed to the desert. The outward appearance was changed, but the inner reality remained the same. The schema was conformed, but the morphe was unchanged. A tank is a tank is a tank, whether green or tan.

There is a danger that people who don't really want to offer themselves wholeheartedly to the Lord for His service in a sacrificial lifestyle will develop a chameleon Christianity that is expert at conforming to situations. In the church it is very churched. Among the faithful it speaks the language of Zion, but in the locker room the language of Sodom. In the sanctuary it does unto others as it would be done unto, but in the business world it does others in before being done in!

Such people feel a great desire to be in the mainstream, to be where the action is, to be part of the flow. They have a desperate need to be accepted, a paralyzing fear of being seen as oddballs.

Their solution is to paint themselves in the colors of the changing scene and be camouflaged into acceptance, fitting in with the crowd.

God says, "I don't need that. I need people who have been so transformed from the inside by the renewing of their minds that it is clear their lives are Mine. When they're in business, they're clearly Christian businesspeople; when they're in church, they're Christian worshipers. When they're home, they're Christian spouses and parents, and in the locker room everybody knows they are thoroughly Christian athletes."

A Renewed Mind

The transformation that comes from within is the result of a renewed mind that is in touch with eternal truth through the inner working of the Spirit of God. Thomas Oden wrote over twenty years ago, "I am a modern man, still fascinated with the twentieth century . . . although I keep wondering to what depth my soul has been traded away."[10]

Now we have entered the twenty-first century—and just like the century that came before, it is incredibly impressive, and we are incredibly impressionable. The seductive charms and the stirring challenges of "the pattern of this world" can be so compelling that the unrenewed mind may imbibe the errors of the age and buy into the lifestyles of the era without recognizing what is happening. This kind of conformity can be disastrous.

Recently a young leader in our singles ministry told a hushed congregation of the way in which his life had been initially conformed and was now being totally transformed, and he spoke specifically about the renewal of his mind. At age thirteen he joined a youth gang that specialized in drinking and vandalism. By seventeen he had a three-page driving record. With his license revoked, he hitchhiked to California, joined the scene and then returned penniless to Milwaukee. He bought a new nylon rope and tried to hang himself; the rope broke, and he finished up in jail, addicted to cocaine, heroin and alcohol.

Then he heard a simple gospel presentation by a visiting pastor, believed, committed his life and began to be transformed. As he said, "My mind has been renewed by Christ, and He has healed me physically, emotionally, psychologically, legally, financially, relationally—and most of all, spiritually. I have told Him I love Him and will spend the rest of my life serving Him."

A living example of a life transformed and no longer conformed to the patterns of the present age. These, then, are the requests God makes of His children, and the characteristics of the holy lifestyle.

Practical Reasons for God's Requests

God not only surprises us by making requests, but amazingly, He gives His reasons. Here's the first one. Romans 12:1 starts with the word *"Therefore,"* which means that the requests are based on all that has been explained in the first eleven chapters. There we find the great explanation of human need and divine grace, of man's obduracy and God's patience, of secular disaster and eternal provision. It's all there, and it all stems from God's incredible goodness. If you are struggling with responding to the requests of God, I encourage you to study the first eleven chapters of Romans, which Paul summarizes as "the mercies of God."

Many years ago as a young evangelist, I stayed in the home of an elderly widow while conducting a week's meetings in a local church. One night after a meeting in which I had preached on Romans 12:1–2, my hostess said that she had found the message most disturbing. She added that she was reluctant to make a "living sacrifice" of herself.

I suggested, semifacetiously I must admit, that she should take a yellow legal pad, read the first eleven chapters of Romans and make a list of the "mercies of God." I added that a proper understanding of His mercies would serve to deal with her reluctance.

The next morning when I came down for breakfast my hostess, looking decidedly bleary-eyed, said, "I got no sleep last night, and it's your fault!" She went on to explain that she had spent all night "renewing her mind" with the truth of God's Word in Romans chapters 1–11. Then she added quietly, "It did the trick! I'm overwhelmed with His mercy, and I've gladly offered myself without reserve to Him for His purposes."

The second reason is that it is "pleasing to God." If I had time, I'd like to tell you about my children. It would require at least three books. Then I could start on my grandchildren. The more I talked, the more you'd know how pleased I am with them. You'd see me glowing and swelling with pride! The reason I would talk that way about them is that they are "extraordinarily pleasing" to me. That is the word that Paul uses. To give ourselves to the Lord is extraordinarily pleasing to Him. I'm hard pressed to think of a better reason for doing what He asks!

The third reason is that it's our "reasonable service" or our "spiritual worship." The word translated "spiritual" also means "reasonable," and the word translated "worship" also means "service." Have you ever found yourself differentiating between "worship" and "service"? As if worship is something you do on Sunday morning and service is something you do during the week, if you have time? Whatever differentiation we may make in this matter, it is significant that in the biblical view there is much less of a dichotomy. The two are bound up in each other. We serve the Lord as we worship Him on Sunday, and we worship Him as we serve Him in the everyday events.

In the same way there may be an inappropriate dichotomizing of what is "spiritual" and what is "reasonable." To the Western mind, that which is reasonable is often set in marked contrast to that which is spiritual, and vice versa. Many people feel that their lives have a reasonable compartment where they make everyday decisions and a spiritual closet in which religious considerations are stored. To think this way is to develop a dangerous mind-set. It may suggest that the "spiritual" may be unreasonable or irrational; and given our modern rationalistic bias, this all too often leads to decision making and actions which totally disregard spiritual principles.

To understand the renewed mind is to recognize the benevolent influence of spiritual principles upon the rational, reasonable processes, and at the same time to appreciate how the life of faith not only lends itself to careful Spirit-guided thought, but requires that we worship and love God with our mind as well as our heart and strength. No wedge should be driven between spiritual worship and reasonable service; both are expected of us by God Himself. It is illuminating to note, therefore, how "spiritual worship" and "reasonable service" are totally interchangeable terms, and both are related to a holy lifestyle.

Promised Results

But what are the results of all this? God is gracious in telling us in advance. He could have said, "Just trust Me!" But instead He explained that if we do it His way we "will be able to test and approve what God's will is—His good, pleasing, and perfect will." Most believers I know genuinely want God's will to be worked out in their lives, but they are not always sure how to go about it. They should, however, be greatly encouraged when they realize that God says they will practically experience the sheer goodness and appropriateness of His will to the extent they gladly respond to his call to a holy lifestyle. The principle is simple and straightforward. We can summarize as follows:

- Offer yourselves unreservedly to Him.
- Don't go on conforming to your environment—allow God's Spirit to transform you from the inside out.
- This is your reasonable service, the essence of spiritual worship and an appropriate response to God's mercy.
- In addition it pleases God in an extraordinary way.

That's it as far as you're concerned. And God for His part will see that you have every opportunity to prove how good and perfect and acceptable God's will really is.

PRAYER

Dear Lord, as we bow quietly before You, we have to admit that we're much better at accepting You as Savior than acknowledging You as Lord. We're much better at receiving blessings than accepting responsibilities. We're much more open to having You do for us what we want You to do, than being prepared to be what You want us to be.

But You've been getting through to us about what it means to be set apart for You. And we realize that some very definite decisions need to be made. We need to be taking a stand one way or the other. And so we'd like You to know that we will unreservedly commit ourselves to You, that we will seek to so nourish and nurture our lives, that we'll be clearly set apart for You and live a life that is extraordinarily pleasing to You. Then we will discover how good and perfect and acceptable Your will really is. Hear our prayer in Christ's name. Amen.

A PERSONAL NOTE FROM JILL

The word "holiness" doesn't seem to match up with the word "body." One seems so mystical and spiritual, and the other so material. Yet I had not been a Christian very long before I realized my body was the outward expression of the inner reality of my relationship with God.

My tongue, for example, belongs to my body. It is "wagged" in accordance with the impulses I send it from my brain. A wise bard of old said, "Speak that I may see thee!" He did not, interestingly enough, say, "Speak that I may hear thee!" And yet we all know that words tell an honest tale about the man who utters them.

Before I knew Jesus I didn't have a very clean mouth. When I got into the student world, I borrowed their language, thinking it was sophisticated to swear as a matter of course and blaspheme in a "mild" sort of way.

But once the Holy Spirit came into my life, He led me to parts of the holy Scriptures that rebuked such unholy language: "Out of the same mouth come praise and cursing. My brothers, this should not be," James said sternly to me (3:10). And again the words of Jesus, "Let your 'Yes' be 'Yes' and your 'No, No'; anything beyond this comes from the evil one" (Matt. 5:37). Part of the transformation in my speech came as a result of a renewed mind that directed my will to instruct a member of my body to be obedient!

Again, there was a question of what to do with my ears. I

could lend them to gossip or deliberately send a message to my brain to turn my head away and lend them to God!

Then there were my hands. Before conversion they had been busy holding all sorts of sports equipment for personal self-aggrandizement. Later I still played sports, but my hands lifted the phone to invite a non-believing friend to play with me in order that my ears could listen to her troubles and my tongue could tell her about Jesus!

My mind being informed of the directives for my life, I became conformed to His pattern for my life and not the pattern of the world. It was a question of my will directing my body parts to be obedient! This way my lifestyle began to be transformed.

CHAPTER QUESTIONS

1. Define in a paragraph the difference between separation and isolation.

2. Paul tells us not to be conformed to the pattern of this world. Read First John 2:15–17. Find the following four things in these verses and write them in your own words.

   a. A command

   b. A statement

   c. A warning

   d. A promise

   Ask yourself which of the above is most relevant to your immediate situation. Pray about it.

3. Make a list of the things your "body" is doing to serve God. Can you think of one thing you are doing at the moment you could describe as sacrificial?

4. Reread the section under the subhead "Nonconformity," especially the discussion about being a "chameleon" or "camouflaged" Christian. Have you ever felt this could be a description of you? Pray about that and also for others you know who struggle with this.

5. Read a few chapters of Romans 1–11 and make a list of the mercies of God. Then spend time praising Him for them.

6. Living a holy life helps us to discern God's will for our life. If you are seeking His mind on some matter, first search your heart for known sin or disobedience and confess it. Second, yield mind, will and body to do His will. Third, ask Him in prayer to reveal it to you. Fourth, do it!

7

THE HOLY SCRIPTURES

I have revealed You to those whom You gave Me out of the world. They were Yours; You gave them to Me and they have obeyed Your word. Now they know that everything You have given Me comes from You. For I gave them the words You gave Me and they accepted them. They knew with certainty that I came from You, and they believed that You sent Me. I pray for them. I am not praying for the world, but for those You have given Me, for they are Yours. (JOHN 17:6–9)

When I was a boy growing up in England, one of my favorite preachers was an Anglican clergyman named Guy King. I came across one of his books a while ago, long out of print but recently republished. More than fifty years ago, he wrote something that is certainly true of our own day: "In such an age as this, when there is abroad so much loose thinking, lax living and lopsided teaching, few things are so important as that Christians should be men and women of the Bible—stayed on it and steeped in it."[11]

Recent surveys show that more than eight out of ten Americans claim to be Christians, but four out of ten don't know who preached the Sermon on the Mount. Only four out of ten know the names of the four Gospels, and only one out of ten believes that all the Ten Commandments are relevant today. Forty percent believe that only five or fewer of the Commandments are relevant.[12]

We have an interesting situation in America: the population is 80 percent Christian according to the people's own testimonial, but many show little interest in God's Word. They profess to "believe" the Bible, but on a selective basis. If it confirms preconceptions and endorses existing lifestyles, it is acceptable; but if it doesn't fit, then it is rejected or ignored. God's Word is no longer revered as the final authority in matters of faith and practice—the historic Christian position; rather, it is a repository of promises to be claimed if desirable, and commands to be obeyed if not uncomfortable! God's Word is subjected to scrutiny that is both casual and occasional.

The Bible and Holiness

You may be wondering what place a concern about biblical knowledge and application or lack thereof has in a discussion of holiness. The purpose of this chapter is to show that the Bible plays a crucial role in the life of holiness. But what exactly is that role?

In John chapter 17 we have a record of Jesus praying to the Father in the hearing of His disciples. Among other things, this prayer gives us Jesus' evaluation of His ministry. Remember He prayed this immediately prior to being arrested, betrayed, tried and crucified. It's almost as if He was giving the Father an end-of-project report, an account of His stewardship:

I am coming to You now, but I say these things while I am still in the world, so that they may have the full measure of My joy within them. I have given them Your word and the world has hated them, for they are not of the world any more than I am of the world. My prayer is not that You take them out of the world but that You protect them from the evil one. They are not of the world, even as I am not of it. Sanctify them by the truth; Your word is truth. As You sent Me into the world, I have sent them into the world. For them I sanctify Myself that they too may be truly sanctified. (JOHN 17:13-19)

Notice how the Lord Jesus summarized His work down here on earth. In John 17 He said that He had:

- Brought God glory (17:4)
- Revealed God's name (17:6)
- Given the disciples God's Word (17:8, 14)
- Protected the disciples and kept them safe (17:12)
- Sent the disciples into the world (17:18)
- Sanctified Himself for His disciples' sanctification (17:19)

I Have Bought You Glory

The Westminster Catechism tells us that the chief end of man is to glorify God and to enjoy Him forever. If that is the chief purpose of humanity, how much more true was it of the Lord Jesus? He didn't come to teach His own teaching or to establish His own empire, to bolster His own ego or to do His own thing. His overriding objective was to glorify the Father. At the end of His life, He was able to report that this was exactly what He had done. But what does it mean "to bring glory" to God?

Moses desired to see the glory of God (Exod. 33:18); David said "the heavens declare" it (Ps. 19:1); John and his fellow disciples spent three years gazing upon it in the person of Jesus (John 1:14). In this sense the "glory of God" is the display of God's character and person in all its wealth and wonder.

Yesterday my wife and I spent a day set aside for "quiet" with about 370 young people busily involved in mission outreach in trying circumstances. As part of their worship, they sang contemporary choruses—over and over again—as is their usual practice! One of these songs, which was an obvious favorite and sung with great feeling, confessed a variety of longings, including the desire to see the Lord's face, to touch Him, to hear His voice.

While I would not personally use such language, I certainly understand the desires expressed for a deeper, fuller recognition of the person of the living God. This, Jesus said He had provided! He had revealed God's glory!

In Moses' day God's presence was revealed in the pillar of fire and the cloud that accompanied the children of Israel throughout their wilderness journeys. David saw the glory in creation. But the paramount revelation was in Christ, who said, "Anyone who has seen me has seen the Father" (John 14:9).

In our day, in addition to the glory in the creation, we see the wonder of God's person in His self-revelation in Christ recorded in and preserved for us in the pages of the Scriptures. He brings glory to Himself in the way we respond to the revelation in the Word.

I Have Revealed You

Literally He said, "I have revealed Your name to those You gave Me." The name of God is intended to be a description of

His person, His character and His work. So when He said, "I have revealed Your name," He meant, "I have shown people who You are, what You're like and what You're doing."

The Old Testament is full of the various names whereby God revealed Himself, but surely the most endearing name is the one Jesus used repeatedly. He called God "Holy Father" (John 17:11). Jesus taught His disciples to address God as Father in prayer, and ever since it has been a favorite form of address of modern believers. The thought of God as Father is deeply meaningful to many believers who struggle with what they perceive as God's remoteness. While they find His transcendence awe-inspiring but not welcoming, they are drawn to the image of God in His fatherliness. (I recognize, however, that those who have had poor relations with their earthly fathers frequently find it hard to address God as Father.)

The ideal father pities his children. God pities us. As a father carries the little children who are finding the road too hard for them, so the Father supports us when life is hard. As a father disciplines his children, so the Lord disciplines us for our good. These are endearing and encouraging revelations of God's character.

But in our understanding of God as Father, we must not overlook the emphasis Jesus gave to "Holy Father." As we have seen, His holiness distinguishes everything about Him. He is separate, other, distinct, pure; He cannot look upon iniquity; He is awesome. All this serves to strike a degree of reverence and fear in our hearts. So a correct revelation of His name, which was the point of Jesus' ministry, maintains the two in balance. He is the Holy Father. We recognize in Jesus God's transcendence and His holiness, and we rejoice in His immanence, His evident compassion, His deep love. Jesus could truly say that He had brought God glory and revealed God's name to mankind. And as we rejoice in His fatherhood and bow before His holiness, we bring Him glory.

I Have Given Them Your Word

People who live in what we somewhat arrogantly call the most primitive cultures are able to communicate with each other. This means that they can relate to what is going on around them, observe it, formulate ideas about it, invent words to identify their observations and ideas, and then use the words to transmit those ideas to other members of their community. And we call those cultures primitive! Yet there are no animals capable of anything remotely close to these accomplishments.

Anyone going into these cultures with a view to trade or aid or missionary activity will find it necessary to embark on the arduous task of language learning, and that means formulating vocabulary, unearthing rules of grammar and discovering the meanings of idioms and metaphors. All this requires words, for words are integral to communication. If thoughts are to be effectively conveyed to another person, words are the medium of choice.

The Greeks believed that behind the universe there existed some kind of intelligent power—an uncaused Cause or unmoved Mover—who was the reason or explanation of observable phenomena. They gave this entity the name *Logos*.

John started his gospel with the well-known words, "In the beginning was the Word [*Logos*] and the Word was with God and the Word was God" (1:1) and went on later to reveal that this "Word became flesh and dwelt among us," thus identifying Jesus as the Word! So when John used Logos, he was stating that

Jesus was not only the rational intelligence behind all things, but He was also the means of communicating to mankind the hidden thought of God the creator and upholder of the universe. He was the ultimate Word!

There were two ways in which the revealing work of Jesus, the Word, was accomplished: through the words he spoke, conveying the truth that the disciples needed to learn, and through the life He lived, which illustrated the words and graphically portrayed the truth. (In His day there were visual and auditory learners too!) For instance, He taught that He was "the resurrection and the life"—but He amplified this by raising Lazarus from the dead (John 11:25, 43). He said He was "the Bread of life," and He showed what He meant by feeding five thousand families with five loaves and two fishes (John 6:11–12, 48). Words were heard, the Word was seen.

Are you inclined to think how wonderful it would have been to be an eyewitness to Christ, like John and his friends? While we were not afforded that privilege, God did graciously preserve for us an inspired written record of the incarnate Lord Jesus in the written Word.

Of course, words have to be accepted if they are to fulfill their purpose. If I smell smoke, the thought may occur to me, *The house is on fire!* That thought in and of itself will be of no help to people in danger. To convey this hidden idea to the house's occupants, I must utilize a word—probably by shouting "Fire!" The occupants of the house will then hear a word that conveys my thought—but they need to accept its reality and respond by leaving the building, so that they don't end up as cinders.

In the same way, we have the revelation of the hidden God in a Word—the living Christ, and the testimony of Him recorded for us in the Scriptures—which needs to be accepted, deeply known and obeyed. This was all part of the work that the Lord Jesus accomplished in order that He might glorify the Father. Those who accepted and obeyed the Word became His disciples. So Jesus could rightly say, "I have given them your word"—and we can add that He has also made it available to us two thousand years later.

I Have Protected and Sent Them Forth

The Lord reported back to the Father, "I have protected them, I have kept them safe, and I have sent them into the world" (John 17:12, 18). This may seem rather strange. Given that the Lord Jesus was concerned about His few disciples, and given that He realized the world in which they lived was hostile to His purposes, one would have expected Him to say something like, "Now Father, I've done what You've told Me to do. I have glorified You, I revealed Your name, I've given them Your Word, I've got a few people to respond, and now I'm leaving. Let Me take these people with Me, because it will be tough for them to be disciples in this environment."

Instead, He said that in the same way that He had been sent into the world, they should be sent too. He knew that He had come into the world not just to live and die and rise again, but to communicate truth to people and to ensure that the communication of this truth would continue until the end of the age. This meant that those who received the truth would also receive a commission to disseminate it to every people group in the world.

Jesus was perfectly candid about the task before them. He knew only too well that the world was a hostile environment. He was also fully aware of the weaknesses of His disciples. And He anticipated the violent opposition by the Enemy of mankind to the broadcasting of God's truth. They needed to be carefully and adequately prepared for the task before them. He called it being "sanctified"—that is, *made holy* or *set apart* for the work (John 17:17).

I Have Sanctified Myself

The Lord Jesus added something very important: "For them I sanctify Myself, that they too may be truly sanctified" (John 17:19). The Lord Jesus was not asking His disciples to do anything He would not do Himself. In fact, it is because of what He did that He asked them (and us) to be what He wants us to be. What did He do? He sanctified Himself, set Himself apart for the holy Father's service, without reservation. At the end of His life, He could report that He had completed that for which He set Himself apart. "I've glorified You, Father; I've revealed Your name. I've given them Your Word. I've sent them into the world. I've protected them. I've saved them. Father, I have set Myself apart for Your purposes in these people's lives."

There was one piece of unfinished business, of course. He had to die and rise again. In dying on the cross, He would sanctify Himself without reserve, sacrificially setting Himself apart to the Father's purpose and will. Because of that, He felt quite free in expecting those who benefited from His sanctification to be similarly set aside for His purposes.

When I was in my twenties, I enjoyed singing in an exceptionally good choir—the Greenside Choir from Kendal Westmoreland in the north of England. We had a gifted conductor, and under her leadership we won a national championship. Our conductor was in great demand and had a waiting list of students who wanted to pay for her services. But she made a simple commitment to the choir from which, incidentally, she received no remuneration: she set Tuesday nights apart, and she set herself apart for the Greenside Choir.

She had just one very simple expectation of the choir, and it was this: "As I am going to set Tuesdays apart for you, I expect you, if you're going to be part of this choir, to set Tuesdays apart too." She could have said, "I'm going to sanctify myself in order that you sanctify yourselves." That was one of the reasons it was a championship choir. We had leadership that was utterly devoted, which produced followership that was equally devoted. So once again we come back to the point we have reiterated in previous chapters, that holiness is not an optional extra, but is what disciples of Christ are called to.

The World

Jesus did not just review the work that He had done, but He outlined what He was going to do. He was about to send His disciples out into a world which was opposed to the work of God. He explained, "I have given them Your Word, and the world has hated them, for they are not of the world, any more than I am of the world" (17:14).

Over and over in Scripture, "the world" means the prevailing attitude and atmosphere of society which is independent of, and hostile to, God and His purposes. Sometimes this will show up in outright naked aggression. When this happens, the things of God are mercilessly and brutally destroyed.

But more often the world is very sophisticated, very benign and utterly lethal. So when Ted Turner, founder of CNN glibly says, "Let's replace the Ten Commandments with Ten Voluntary Initiatives," that's the world talking. And when eight out of ten Americans say they are Christians, but dismiss the Ten Commandments as irrelevant, that is the world talking in the church!

It was into this environment that Jesus sent His followers. "My prayer is not that you take them out of the world but that you protect them from the evil one" (John 17:15). Jesus knew how important it was for His followers to be "kept" in the world. They were not of the world, and they knew in advance that because the world hated Jesus (as would be evidenced in a few short hours by His rejection and crucifixion) so they could anticipate it would hate them too. Nevertheless, despite the fact that it would be hostile to them, they were to go and minister the Word in it and to it. But it was imperative that they be set apart, clean and fit for the Master's use.

Protected and Projected

But how are Christ's followers to be set apart, kept and used in the Master's service in such a hostile situation? The answer is found in the prayer, "Father, sanctify them by the truth; Your Word is truth" (John 17:17). In other words, the *written Word* (which records the spoken word and gives a historical account of the Living Word, who is the revelation of God) is *His Truth* (when applied to disciples' lives)—it sets them apart, projects them into His service, protects them, empowers them, instructs them, encourages them, keeps them clean and fit for His use.

God's Word, the Bible, is designed to protect us from evil, from the Evil One. I remember seeing an old Bible in which somebody had written on the front page, "This book will keep you from sin, but sin will keep you from this book." That's a good statement. The Book will keep us from sin, not when it sits on a shelf but when it is read, marked, learned and inwardly digested, believed, trusted and obeyed. It will not keep us and empower us if we simply look at the Ten Commandments and decide which ones we agree with and which we can ignore.

Recently a young couple told me, "We had no idea that what we were doing in our lives was wrong until you told us about holiness. But now as God's Word has become clear to us, we realize that what we were doing was evil. We've been deeply convicted about this, we have repented of it, we've confessed it to God, and we've turned from it."

You know what was happening? The process of sanctification was taking place in their lives. They were "cleaning up their act." They were being separated from the world of which they had been a part, and now instead of being part of it, they were learning to be in it but not of it, in order to be of service to it.

The Word of Truth

If there is such a thing as truth, there is error. If there's such a thing as light, there is dark. If there's such a thing as right, there is wrong. There are those who want to persuade us otherwise. They reject the idea that there is absolute truth—and ironically, they reject it absolutely! The anchor of the soul that will keep you from error is God's Word. His Word is truth. So if we are to be of service to God, we need to project truth in the midst of error. There is considerable error abroad concerning God, humankind, life and death. There is no shortage of confusion deep in the soul and written plainly on the faces of our contemporaries. There are endless counterfeit "gospels" and a veritable smorgasbord of philosophies available to a searching society.

It's a wild world, it's a wicked world, and it's a worried world out there; and it's a world that deserves to hear the truth as it is in Jesus. That is the task of the sanctified ones.

You may be thinking, "Who in his right senses would stick his neck out in a hostile world and tell it what it does not want to know? Who would live righteously among the unrighteous, knowing that the unrighteous will get upset? Who would speak truth in the midst of error, knowing that error doesn't want the truth?"

I understand these questions, as well as the feelings of trepidation and the sense of inadequacy behind them. But something can happen in our lives which triumphs over reservations and reluctance. That "something" is the realization that the Savior set Himself apart to set us apart to be witnesses to the Word of God, the truth. When this truth is released in people's lives, it accomplishes great and wonderful things, to God's glory.

The Lord Jesus said, "If you hold to My teaching, you are really My disciples. Then you will know the truth, and the truth will set you free" (John 8:31–32). How many times have you seen "The truth will set you free" quoted? On university libraries you see it engraved in stone, taken out of context and made to mean something Jesus never meant at all.

The people who heard Jesus say it objected, "We were never slaves to anybody; why do we need to be set free?" To which He responded, "If you commit sin, you're the slaves of sin."

What was the freedom He was talking about? Freedom from sin. How does this freedom come? It comes from the Word that sets you free. How? By responding to the Word, by becoming His disciple. If you accept His Word and become His disciple, you'll know the truth and the truth will set you free from the evil that will disqualify you from being set apart for God's service.

So the work of Christ is very straightforward. He was separated from the world, but sent into it to be of service to it, in order that He might prepare us to be separated from the world and sent into it to be of service to it. A major part of this is accomplished through the work of the Word of God in our hearts as we respond to it in glad obedience and say, "Lord, deal with me, cleanse me where necessary, correct me when necessary, thrust me out into Your service when necessary. But make Your Word take root in my life and bear fruit through my life."

PRAYER

Thank You, Father, for the ministry of the Lord Jesus. Thank You for His end-of-term report. Thank You that He clearly enunciated that He had concluded that which You gave Him to do. And thank You that He came to be set apart for Your service in order to produce people who'll be set apart for His service.

Lord, very often we don't want to be Yours, we want to be ours. And very often we don't want to be rid of the things that would be a hindrance, because we have found them a delight. That is why it was necessary for the Lord Jesus to pray that down through the ages men and women and boys and girls will be sanctified by Your Word, because Your Word is truth.

We pray that as we have given attention to the teaching of Your Word, we would not allow it to disappear into thin air. We ask the Spirit who inspired it to apply it to our lives, that in increasing measure we will be separated from the world in order to be of service to the world. This we pray in Christ's name. Amen.

A PERSONAL NOTE FROM JILL

Shortly after becoming a believer, I discovered an interesting fact—that I had not changed overnight! It was a bit like cleaning out my garage. In our home everything that didn't have a place found itself in the garage. As long as I could put the door down on the whole awful mess, I lived on happily without bothering too much about it.

But the day of reckoning had to come. The day dawned when I put the door up and began to haul everything in sight out into the driveway in order to sort it all out. After a lot of hard work, I was tired. I still had the dark corners and the high shelves to work on, places where boxes contained junk I didn't even remember bothering to store away.

My great temptation was to leave well enough alone and wait until we moved. No one would know what lay in the dark recesses of the garage if I put clean boxes in front of the mess. And so that is what I did. But it didn't work, because I knew what lay in the cobwebbed corners and on the high shelves. And I was not at peace.

What a parallel to so much of my Christian living. To all intents and purposes, things can look perfectly fine at first glance. But God's Holy Spirit worked on my conscience and convicted me of those old dusty boxes I never really cleared out.

One of those boxes in my life was the box of worry. The Word says, "Whatever is not of faith is sin." I learned that worry and faith are diametrically opposed to each other. Worry is a lack of faith that God is sovereign. Worry tries to turn me into a little god, organizing my world. I found myself trying to answer my own prayers. God knew, and I knew, that my worry box had never really been dealt with. Somehow it didn't seem to be as "unholy" as the bad-language box or the temper chest.

Yet sanctification meant I must allow God to deal with all my boxes, not just the ones near at hand or the ones I had the strength or will to deal with. Otherwise I would grieve God's Holy Spirit who lived in me.

This box needed time, patience and sorting out. First I had to give in to God and let Him decide what to do with it. My worry box was the fullest and largest box in the whole of my garage, and I didn't know where to begin. So I began to worry about my worry box. I worried my way through my single days, married days, good days and bad days, troubled days and days when there wasn't a cloud in my sky. (I worried where the clouds had all gone and when they were coming back!) I continued to ignore Matthew 6, saying to myself, "I'm not worrying about clothes, food or drink, but rather about 'spiritual' things, family things, good things," as if this gave me permission to go ahead and produce an ulcer.

God showed me that worry is unholy. First, I admitted I worried. I stopped being in denial and faced up to the grim fact that I was a worrier rather than a truster! Second, each time I began to worry I confessed it. If the Bible says, "Whatever is not of faith is sin," it means it and I was sinning. What's more, this sin was spoiling my fellowship with the Lord. Third, I repented, changed my mind about worrying, and turned my will toward trusting.

My worry box was so big it has taken years and years to empty out, but it is getting emptier, and now I realize that the holier we become, the less worrying we will do! I learned above all that there is such a thing as legitimate concern, and it needs to be differentiated from illegitimate anxiety.

For example, one day I was in a small plane with three of my good friends. A man in our congregation had offered to fly us to Chicago to purchase furniture for the parsonage. We got caught in a terrible storm. Sweat was rolling down our pilot's face as he was turned away from the airport. He began to look at his gas gauge and measure distances.

The four mothers in the plane looked at each other. All of us were battling fear. If there was ever a time to have legitimate concern, it was now.

In my case illegitimate panic was kept at bay by my theology, faith and prayer. I, who had an inordinate fear of flying, knew I would not go to heaven one moment before I was meant to. It surely looked as though this might be the moment—and yet, even on that occasion, I was able to trust in the sovereign God and put my life in His hands.

Obviously, I lived to tell the tale. It is often the little worry boxes of life rather than the big ones that take all my energy; but big or little and one by one, they must be tackled in the power of the Lord. I cannot be holy if they are not.

CHAPTER QUESTIONS

1. Reread John White's description of holiness (near the beginning of Chapter 6).

    a. Which description have you agreed with in the past?

    b. What words or phrases would you add to indicate your own perceptions of holiness?

    c. When you hear the phrase "sacrificial lifestyle," what springs to mind?

2. Read Luke 1:26–38.
    a. Could Christ have been born if Mary had only offered her soul and her spirit?

    b. How is she a good example of Romans 12:1–2?

3. God gives us His good reasons for living a holy life. They are the mercies of God.

a. Take a note pad and read fifteen minutes worth of Romans 1–11 (more if you wish). When you've finished, write a short note to God about your personal response to the mercies of God.

b. Make a list of all the things that please you about the person you love the most. Then ask yourself how many of those characteristics you recognize in your own relationship with God.

c. Think about your reasonable service and your spiritual worship. What one thing will you try to change as you think of these two phases?

8

Lift Holy Hands in Prayer

I urge, then, first of all, that requests, prayers, intercession, and thanksgiving be made for everyone—for kings and all those in authority, that we may live peaceful and quiet lives in all godliness and holiness. This is good, and pleases God our Savior, who wants all men to be saved and to come to a knowledge of the truth. For there is one God and one mediator between God and men, the Man Christ Jesus, who gave Himself as a ransom for all men—the testimony given in its proper time. And for this purpose I was appointed a herald and an apostle—I am telling the truth, I am not lying—and a teacher of the true faith to the Gentiles. I want men everywhere to lift up holy hands in prayer, without anger or disputing. (1 Tim. 2:1–8)

There was a time when, if I was asked to define holiness, I would probably have talked about sinlessness, moral purity and similar topics. But further study led me to conclude that the primary meaning of holiness is *separate*-ness, set *apart*-ness or *distinctive*-ness as we have seen thus far. Remember pots, pans, pieces of real estate and certain buildings were declared holy—

things with no moral components in their make-up. However, to associate holiness with moral purity is perfectly legitimate. It is not correct to see the primary meaning of holiness in this light, but it is a significant secondary meaning that we should recognize and embrace.

God, as we have seen, is holy, and we know that in His separateness; He is separate from sin. We are told to be holy because He is holy, and that certainly means among other things that, in recognition of His separateness from all that defiles and degrades, diminishes and destroys, we too should take steps to develop and maintain practical moral holiness in our lives. In fact, one of the obvious evidences of our "set-apart-ness" will be our rejection of what is anathema to God and all too common in the world—and painfully prevalent in the lives of those who are without Christ.

The question is how we are to maintain this kind of life. In Chapter Seven we noted that paying attention to God's Word plays a significant role. The Lord Jesus prayed for the disciples and asked the Father to sanctify them through the Word, which is truth. As we apply God's Word to our hearts in the power of the Holy Spirit, our lives are cleansed and kept clean so that they might be pure and usable in His service. The psalmist asked, "How can a young man keep his way pure?" And he found the answer immediately: "By living according to your Word" (119:9).

The Call to Prayer

Now we will take a look at how prayer plays a part in developing a holy life as well. In his letter to Timothy, Paul wrote, "I urge then first of all that requests, prayers, intercession, and thanksgiving be made for everyone" (1 Tim. 2:1). Prayer was high on Paul's list of priorities for Timothy and the church at Ephesus where he ministered.

If you were to go around your church congregation and say, "What do you think ought to be the top priority in this church?" you probably would receive a variety of answers. Worship! Evangelism! Teaching! Fellowship! Support groups! Music! These are all legitimate aspects of church life and ministry. But the apostle Paul said "first of all" there must be prayer, and he either meant prayer is the first thing I need to discuss with you, or prayer is the number one priority! Either way, in his mind prayer was vitally important.

Perhaps it would be helpful at this point if we asked ourselves a couple of questions: "Is prayer a priority in the life of the community of believers to which I belong? Is it a priority for me?" We'll see the importance of these questions as we go along.

Notice two words that Paul used in conjunction with prayer. In verse 1, *urge* and in verse 8, *want*; both are strong encouragement words. Obviously, Paul felt deeply about prayer and wanted Timothy and the Ephesians to be encouraged in their prayer lives. Most people I know admit that they too need encouragement in this dimension of spiritual life because they have problems with prayer. But why is this so?

Perhaps one reason is that many of us are practical, pragmatic people, interested in the bottom line, and we find it difficult to see the bottom line of prayer. We are inclined to spend our time and energy on things with a more measurable effectiveness. Another reason is that we are very active people. Life is busy, and there are so many things to do. But when we pray, we have to pull out of activity and busyness to get quiet and spend time listening and talking to the Lord. This mind-set was captured cleverly in a cartoon I saw recently. A church secretary, having burst into the pastor's office unannounced, found him on his knees in prayer and said, "Oh, good—you're not busy!"

Another problem that is real but rarely voiced is that many people don't really know how prayer works. They hear that God is sovereignly accomplishing His eternal purposes, that absolutely nothing will thwart Him and that everything will come out as He planned it in the end. So if God is going to do what He is going to do anyway, they wonder what possible difference their prayers can make.

Let me give you an example that may shed a little light on the way prayer can become more effective in our lives. When I was a banker, one of my responsibilities was to look after the safe deposit boxes that some of our customers rented from us. In these boxes our customers kept such things as insurance policies, legal documents, jewelry—and in some cases, we rather suspected, the cash they hadn't declared to the federal government. Naturally, they didn't want us poking around in their treasures, so they had a key for their safe deposit box. But we kept the key to the vault, where the safe deposit boxes were stored. The only way anyone could get into a safe deposit box was if the banker first opened the vault and the owner opened the safe deposit box. It took two keys.

Let me suggest to you that God has a key in the lock of His will which He is always ready to turn, but He's given us the key of prayer. He says, "I'm turning My key in the lock. Now I've given you the responsibility and the privilege of turning your key in the other lock. When you do, My power will be released and My purposes will come to fruition in the world." God calls us into a cooperative ministry. He, for reasons known only to

Himself, has determined that it takes two keys to release His purposes in this world.

Of course, somebody might ask, "Why in the world did God decide to do it that way?" We'll have to ask Him that one day. But He was certainly paying us a compliment by involving us in His plans. We can only content ourselves with the belief that "the secret things belong to the Lord our God, but the things revealed belong to us and to our children forever" (Deut. 29:29).

There are things God has chosen to reveal to us and they are our precious possession. One of them is prayer and our need to be occupied in this spiritual activity! We can ask questions about the mysteries of prayer that we will never be able to answer. But there are things about prayer that He has revealed to us, and these become our responsibility.

The big question is, "Assuming that God is already turning the key of His purposes, am I turning my key in order that His purposes and His power might be released in my area of influence?" When we think of it in these terms, we can begin to understand why prayer is a priority and why the apostle urged and encouraged the people to join him in prayer.

The Practice of Prayer

The apostle used four specific words to describe different aspects of prayer. They are *requests*, *prayers*, *intercession* and *thanksgiving*.

The word *requests* stems from a sense of need. I recognize a need for divine intervention in this world, and on that basis I come to God.

The word *prayers* denotes an approach either to a person or to God, but in the New Testament the word is used exclusively to describe an approach to God. Prayer addresses God as One who is interested and concerned about the human situation.

The word *intercession* contains the specialized sense of entering into the presence of a king and submitting a petition. A century ago John Newton wrote a hymn about prayer. The second verse says:

> Thou art coming to a King;
> Large petitions with thee bring;
> For His grace and power are such,
> None can ever ask too much.[13]

Intercession means that with a sense of need I address the King of kings and the Lord of lords, who is intimately involved in the concerns that I've addressed to Him.

The word *thanksgiving* means that as on the one hand I recognize the privilege of petition, on the other hand I recognize the responsibility of praise. I need to incorporate the requesting and the praising. I praise God for who He is and for the incredible privilege of being allowed to address Him in prayer. I give thanks for all that He has done, I praise Him for all that He's promised to do, and I praise Him in advance for the way that He will respond to my praying. These are the elements of prayer that must be a priority in our lives. I look at prayer this way:

P stands for *Praise*. I address myself to God, but I'm not talking just about me, I'm not coming in with a shopping list. I am filling my mind with Him in praise and thanksgiving. That's where prayer starts. As soon as I concentrate on Him, I'm reminded of the deficiencies in myself, and this leads to the next step:

R stands for *Repentance*. It is only when I have praised Him and come to repentance that I'm in the right attitude to come before the King with my large petitions.

A stands for *Asking.* As I have praised Him, as I have repented, I am much more likely to pray rightly as I request His intervention in the lives of others.

Y stands for *Yourself.* After the praising, repenting and asking, it is appropriate to get around to talking about "yourself." Please notice the order is P-R-A-Y. If you get it the other way around (Y-A-R-P), it's not *PRAYing*, it's *YARPing*, and therein lies the problem for many people.

Incentives to prayer

Notice the wonderful incentive to prayer at this particular point. After he had encouraged Timothy to pray, Paul added, "This is good and pleases God our Savior" (1 Tim. 2:3). What greater incentive to prayer could there be than the reminder that God is delighted to hear His people pray? But why would praying please God? For one thing, it's a matter of obedience. To pray is to obey, and obedience pleases the Father. For another reason, if we recognize that praying is cooperating with God in the unfolding of His divine eternal plan, we know our willing cooperation is well pleasing to Him. Third, if we're praising and praying correctly, we will be doing one of the most unselfish things of which we are capable.

Praising God is anything but self-centered; it is God-centered. And interceding on behalf of others is anything but self-centered; it is others-centered. These attitudes do not come naturally, and when they begin to appear, they are clear evidences of spiritual growth. God loves to see us growing and maturing in these ways.

The Content of Prayer

The scope of the prayer that Paul advocates is immense. "I urge, then, first of all, that requests, prayers, intercession, and thanksgiving be made for everyone" (2:1). Occasionally I meet people who say, "I don't know where I fit in the church. I don't know my role." I tell them, "If you don't know where you fit and you don't know your role, pray!" The church can use all the praying she can get, because somehow or other we are called to cover "everyone." Now let's limit that a little because it is rather overwhelming to be asked to pray for everyone! How about everyone we know? That narrows it down somewhat! Just think of what could happen if we turned the key in the lock for all the people we know. We could do that!

A few days ago I was up very early. I went out to see what the weather was like and walked around our subdivision. Everything was quiet; people were still asleep. It was about quarter to six, and as I walked past each unit, I found myself praying for the people inside. As I did so, the thought occurred to me, *I wonder if anybody's prayed for these people before? I wonder if anybody has turned the key in the lock for them?*

Let's narrow the target area down even more. How about praying for some special people God specifically brings to your attention? Having said, "everyone," the apostle identified three specific groups.

Unbelievers

Paul said that prayer "pleases God our Savior." Obviously, prayer is effective only if the one to whom the prayer is addressed is able to hear, is capable of answering and is willing to do so. Some people pray with great fervency to a block of wood, but it serves no useful purpose as far as answers go. The one to whom we pray is called "God our Savior." Paul immediately amplified this description in a typical digression. God our Savior "wants all men to be saved and to come to a knowledge of the truth. For there is one God and one mediator between God and men, the Man Christ Jesus, who gave Himself as a ransom for all men" (2:3–5)

God is specifically concerned about the salvation of all people. This is clearly demonstrated in that the Lord Jesus gave Himself a ransom for all people. The purposes and desires of God are all-embracing. Christ's death on the cross is relevant to all people. We are familiar with the term *ransom*. It means to pay the price to deliver a slave from bondage. Paul used the expression in this passage to stress the fact that it is "on behalf of" and "instead of" other people that Christ died. It was "instead of" and "on behalf of" people who need to be saved because they were incapable of saving themselves. This being the message committed to the church, we should be concerned enough to pray that the message of salvation might go out to the people who need to hear it. We should be asking ourselves the very simple question, "To what extent am I praying intelligently, persistently and consistently for the salvation of the people I know?" That is a ministry in which all of us could and should be involved.

You may be thinking, "Hold it just a minute. This idea that God wants everybody to be saved sounds like universalism to me! What about election and predestination and all those good theological ideas?"

I'm glad you brought that up! I was concerned about that too; so I checked up on John Calvin, well known as he is for his emphasis on divine sovereignty. This is what he said, "Since, therefore, He intends the benefits of His death to be common to all, those who hold a view that would exclude any from the hope of salvation do Him an injury." Like John Calvin, we must be careful not to consciously or subconsciously "exclude any," and we should be at pains to include many in our prayers.

It follows quite naturally that a prayerful concern for unbelievers will include specific prayer for those whose lives are particularly devoted to the task of reaching the unreached. Those who live and work in spiritually dark and difficult places are most keenly aware of their need for prayer support. Surely one of the most needed and effective ministries available to new believers is to pray for those who have traveled to the "regions beyond" to reach people who desperately need the message.

Yesterday I received word from two young friends of mine working in the slums of Manila, Philippines. They wrote, "We are in a battle. It's a hard and dangerous situation where things happen so quickly that there's hardly time to pray before it's too late. So keep on praying for us continually."

Those in Authority

Paul also urged prayer for "kings and all those in authority." Since Nero was the Caesar at the time Paul was writing, this is a rather surprising statement. He knew from personal experience that those in authority can either make people's lives a misery or grant them a chance to live peacefully and productively. So he said, "Let's pray for people in authority that they would make it possible for us to serve the living and true God freely and effectively."

Such freedom is nonexistent in some countries even today. In the Western World our religious freedoms are guaranteed. But notice something important here. Paul did not say, "Pray that we might have good political leaders so that we can have a peaceful and quiet life, so we can be comfortable and secure without interruption." He encouraged prayer for those in positions of leadership with a view to the people being free to "lead peaceful and quiet lives in all godliness and holiness" (2:2). One thing I love about the Anglican Church is that they take this admonition seriously and regularly pray for the Queen. In the American church I rarely hear prayers for the President—particularly if he is from the "other party"!

The problem is that when we have a quiet and peaceful situation, we tend to settle down and enjoy the quiet and the peace. In fact, the church often does far better under persecution than it does in times of quiet and peace! Why is this? Because quiet and peace so easily produce an environment in which believers become wrapped up in their personal enjoyment, to the detriment of spiritual growth and vigorous mission activity. But tough times tend to prod us into deeper fellowship with the Lord.

We should not be reluctant to pray for leadership that creates a quiet and peaceful environment, but when these gifts are granted, they should not be indulged, but utilized to produce lives of *godliness* and *holiness*.

These two words are interesting. According to Eusebius, the word godliness means "reverence toward the one and only God, and the kind of life that He would wish us to lead." Holiness is defined by R.C. Trench as "a grace and a dignity, not lent by earth . . . [which] without demanding it, challenges and inspires reverence."[14]

In other words, we should pray for people in authority so that we might be free to develop lives of dignity and quality that, without demanding it, will inspire respect and challenge people to listen to what we have to say.

No doubt believers will continue to have political preferences based on personal needs, priorities and interests. Elected officials and unelected leaders are prone to steer societies in paths which believers do not wish to travel. This can often lead to acrimony, anger and activism, which limits prayer to "Get rid of the rascals, O Lord!" Paul's approach is totally different and far more appropriate. And don't forget—*Nero* was running the show!

Believers

Do you know any believers who could use some prayer with reference to godliness and holiness? Of course you do—in fact, we could all use some! Prayer that believers will be interested in holiness, that they will understand holiness, that they will pursue holiness—much prayer is needed for these concerns. Prayer that churches will put holiness in their strategic planning, that pastors will put it in their regular preaching, that counselors will factor it into their therapy, that young people will be introduced to it in their youth groups—all these topics should become part of believers' prayers. Concerns relating to spiritual revival as well as worries about eternal survival should be high on the agenda.

Prayerful believers know how to concentrate on requests dealing with sickness, joblessness, bereavement, marital discord and numerous other ills that are so often the unhappy lot of believers and unbelievers alike. Not infrequently, the requests center on solutions and alleviation of the problems which is, of course, understandable. But it is good to remember that life's vicissitudes frequently present an opportunity for spiritual growth and maturity not available elsewhere. Prayer should therefore focus not only on the problem and the solution, but also on the possibilities for godliness and holiness to flourish in the unpromising soil of adversity.

The Characteristics of Those Who Pray

"I want men everywhere to lift up holy hands in prayer without anger or disputing" (2:8), added the apostle. In some fellowships, "to lift or not to lift" (usually during times of praise) is an issue! Some people love to do it, and some people hate them doing it, particularly if it blocks their vision. Some who do it look down on those who don't, and some who don't think those who do it are weird! Whatever we may think about the contemporary practice, it is very obvious that in biblical times it was normal to lift up the hands in prayer.

In days gone by it was customary to say, "Every head bowed and every eye closed. Now let us pray!" Where does it say that in the Bible? In some churches you kneel to pray. A case can be made for that practice. Paul specifically said, "For this reason I kneel before the Father" (Eph. 3:14). But I'm afraid that no case can be made biblically for sitting down, chewing gum and looking around during prayer—none whatsoever!

So as far as the culture of Bible times was concerned, it was normative to lift up one's hands. It was a symbolic action intended to convey an inner reality. In lifting up his hands, the person praying was saying, "Lord, I'm reaching out to You." That is pretty graphic, isn't it? The upstretched arms and open hands portrayed, "Look, Lord, my hands are clean and empty. I'm not hanging on to anything inappropriate."

Of course, all symbolism can degenerate into meaninglessness. But when actions portray attitudes, they can be powerful. So if you lift up hands when you pray, make sure they are holy hands—open, eager, unencumbered. The prophet Isaiah said that God was not impressed with the people of Israel, because the hands they lifted up in prayer were covered with blood. They were going through outward motions unrelated to and even contradictory to inner reality, and so God refused to listen to their prayers.

Whether or not we literally lift up our hands in prayer is secondary, but what goes on in the heart is primary. We do not come before the Lord in prayer harboring things in our lives that have no business there. We do not come before Him with unconfessed sin. We are to come into His presence "by the blood of Jesus . . . our hearts sprinkled to cleanse us from a guilty conscience and having our bodies washed with pure water" (Heb. 10:19–22).

One of the reasons prayers go "unanswered" is that they are presented with unprepared hearts. So we see "holy hands" prayer is linked to "prayer without anger and disputing." If my attitude is warped and twisted by anger, how can the Spirit of God lead me to pray correctly? If I'm living in the middle of disputes, and if I am governed by doubt as to what I stand for and where I want to go with my life, how can I quiet my heart in prayer before the Lord?

There has to be preparation of the heart and mind in tune with the Lord for prayer to be effective. Another word for that is holiness. So we see the way in which holiness and prayer are related. Effective praying reaches to the throne with "holy hands," with a great longing for holiness to become part and parcel of the life of those near and dear, far and unknown.

PRAYER

In the name of the Lord Jesus we come into Your presence. Our world is full of incredible needs. We know that You're longing to see people saved, and we know that You're ready to move into their lives. For reasons known only to Yourself, You've given us the privilege and responsibility of cooperating with You in Your work.

We ask that You teach us to pray. We ask that You help us to pray as we ought, for the things that we should. We ask that Your power might be released in and through our lives, and in our fellowship life in a way that we have not seen before. We ask that the turmoil of our world might be stilled so that men and women worldwide might seek after You, to the end that they would perfect holiness in the fear of God. Amen.

A PERSONAL NOTE FROM JILL

Paul said, "I want men everywhere to lift up holy hands in prayer, without anger and disputing" (1 Tim. 2:8). Holy prayer or wholehearted praying, the sort that produces the right sort of God response to our fervent requests, depends on conditions being fulfilled. Two of those conditions are "without anger or disputing."

I have discovered that anger does not help my prayer life. In fact, if I am mad at someone, I find it almost impossible to pray for that person. I glance upward at my holy hands and see clenched fists! And it doesn't help to have some well-meaning friend say, "If you are mad at someone, pray for him or her; that will change your attitude!" How, I ask myself, can I pray if I am so angry with this person? Anger needs to be dealt with first.

The same goes for disputing. The word has a sense of inner doubt and conflict. If I am muddled up internally about a situation that I find myself in, this could perhaps lead to angry exchanges with the very people I am supposed to be helping or praying for.

For me, prayer has always been a grand place to be. I have

enjoyed the intimate comfort of God's presence in prayer as much as any spiritual exercise. To be still and know that He is God, that He is there, and that we together can "connect" in such a way that I will never be the same, is quite thrilling.

On one occasion, however, I found myself boiling inside. We served a vibrant youth mission, and my husband, along with other staff members, traveled extensively. I became angry at his long absences from home—the empty "Daddy space" at bedtimes; the fact that other people's kids had the lion's share of my husband's time, energy and attention. I became angry for our sons, David and Peter—I always seemed to be the only single parent watching their soccer matches.

I looked long and hard at my prayer life and discovered a huge vacuum of intercessory prayer. It had been a while since I had wept on my knees for the rough, tough youngsters we were working with. I realized with a jolt it had been months since I had prayed for the staff as they traveled and preached. I didn't want to, because I was filled with personal anger and confusion.

In another situation when I felt angry, I confided in a close friend and asked her to pray for me so I could get my attitude straightened out. I also asked her to pray for the person I was angry with. Then I began to talk to God about my feelings seething just below the surface. I spent time being quiet, saying nothing, trying to open my mind to His still small voice. I asked Him to bring Scripture to my mind that would help me.

As I talked it all over with God, trying to look at my problem first, I began to have a clearer look at the other side of the issue—her side! At last I was able to pray "around" the situation at hand and finally focused on my adversary.

I discovered that some of my anger was legitimate, and it was all right to allow myself to be indignant in the right manner without getting into a rage. Some of my anger, however, was illegitimate and, like all sin, had to be confessed and put behind me. Then and only then could I lift up holy hands in prayer.

It was years until that particular problem was finally dealt with, but my prayers weren't hindered anymore, and I was at rest being able to accept a less-than-ideal relationship as I waited on God for prayer to be answered. Prayer is a place where God clarifies situations, and it also links us to a God who not only changes the "prayer" but also works out His sovereign purposes, allowing us through holy intercession to be part of the process.

CHAPTER QUESTIONS

1. Read First Timothy 2:8. Ask yourself if anger and confusion are preventing you from praying effectively. Ask God to speak directly to you from the Scriptures. Then spend some time in one of the Epistles, expecting a principle or precept to speak to your need.

2. Circle the reason you struggle with the discipline of personal prayer. Then read the reference next to the reason you have circled.

   a. Active, not passive personality (Luke 10:38–41)

   b. Lack of discipline and time mismanagement (10:38–41)

   c. Busyness (Mark 1:35; Luke 5:16)

   d. Ignorance of the principles of prayer (James 1:5)

   e. No suitable place to pray (Matt. 6:6)

   f. Don't know what to say (6:7–19)

3. Fill in the acrostic with personal praise and prayer needs.

    *P*raise—things you want to thank God for

    *R*epent—things you are sorry about

    *A*sk for others—people you need to pray for (believers and
        unbelievers)

    *Y*ourself—items that concern you at the moment

    Spend some time working through the acrostic in prayer.

4. Spend a quiet period thinking about the words "godliness"
    and "holiness," and what they mean.

5. Borrow the prayer at the end of Chapter 8 and make it your
    own.

9

Worship the Lord in the Beauty of Holiness

Sing to the Lord, all the earth;
  proclaim his salvation day after day.
Declare his glory among the nations,
  His marvelous deeds among all peoples.
For great is the Lord and most worthy of praise;
  he is to be feared above all gods.
For all the gods of the nations are idols,
  but the Lord made the heavens.
Splendor and majesty are before him;
  strength and joy in his dwelling place.
Ascribe to the Lord, O families of nations,
  ascribe to the Lord glory and strength,
  ascribe to the Lord the glory due His name.
Bring an offering and come before Him;
  worship the Lord in the splendor of His holiness.

(1 Chron. 16:23–29)

So far we have recognized that God is holy, that He calls His people to be holy and that we need a considerable amount of help in this regard, help that is to be found in Scripture and in prayer. In this chapter we will think particularly about how worship plays a major part in the life of holiness, as we look into the phrase used by David—"Worship the Lord in the splendor of His holiness," or "in the beauty of holiness" (1 Chron. 16:29). David was inspired to call God's people to worship because of a momentous event in their history—the arrival of the ark of the covenant in Jerusalem, the City of David. The psalm he wrote for the occasion was an expression of celebration for himself and a call to participation for the people.

You may not be as familiar with what the Bible teaches about the lost ark as with the way it was portrayed in *Raiders of the Lost Ark*. There is a very tenuous connection between the biblical story and the popular movie. The fact that the ark was lost is totally accurate, but I'm afraid the similarity between the movie and the biblical account ends there! Let me remind you of what the Bible says about the ark of God, or the ark of the testimony, or the ark of the covenant, as it was variously called.

Worship and the Ark of the Covenant

Human beings were created to be dependent. We were wired up that way. It is an absolute impossibility for us to live in total independence of other things and other people. God ordained this right from the very beginning of creation. Because we are created dependent, we need to be looking away all the time to something or someone beyond and other than ourselves.

We don't need to learn this—it's an instinctive and intrinsic part of human experience. Anthropologists confirm that wherever they go, they discover that human beings recognize these inbuilt desires and set about dealing with them in a wide variety of ways. As a result, many different rituals, traditions and expressions include recognition of something other than themselves. This recognition may include calls on this entity to come to their aid or it may incorporate ways of placating what are deemed to be this being's malevolent purposes.

Now that to which they look, that which becomes central and dominates their lives, is the object of worship. This being so, it is no surprise that God is looking for people to worship Him. Not, I hasten to add, because He needs our worship, but because we, being created dependent and constitutionally inclined to worship, need to be worshiping the only One who can meet our needs, merit our adoration and answer our prayers. Man's chief end is to glorify God and enjoy Him forever!

God revealed His intentions for humanity through His dealings with the children of Israel through the centuries. This was not because He regarded them as being special, and it was certainly not intended to be exclusive. He worked in them and through them for the good of all peoples. In the history of Israel, there are clear indications as to what God had in mind for humans in the area of worship. He brought the children of Israel out of Egypt, delivering them from the bondage of the Egyptians. He led them across the sea and took them to the wilderness where they stopped at Mount Sinai. There He reminded them of a covenant that He had made with Abraham.

Simply stated, the covenant was a commitment that said, in effect, "I'm going to be your God, which means I will care for you and protect you; I'll lead and guide you; I will provide for you. The response I expect from you is your loving, trusting obedience." That was the covenant. God took the initiative and the children of Israel responded.

Their loving obedience was to be shown in many ways, including worship. So God gave them specific instructions concerning a worship center. As they were nomadic people passing through the wilderness, it had to be mobile and suitable for the desert. So He instructed them to build a tent or tabernacle. It was to have a courtyard within which the main tent would stand. The tent itself was divided into two sections. First was the holy place and then the most holy place or the holy of holies.

In the holy of holies there was to be one particular piece of furniture—the ark of the covenant. It was a box about four feet by two feet by two feet which could have been easily overlooked, except that it was overlaid with pure gold. It had a lid called the atonement cover, which included the figures of two cherubim. Their faces were toward each other, and their wings met over the atonement cover. In the ark were placed the two tablets on which the Ten Commandments were engraved, along with a pot of manna—the miraculous wilderness food, and Aaron's famous budding rod.

God then gave instructions concerning their worship practice. First, they were to make the ark, put into it the Ten Commandments, place on it the cover of atonement, and there He promised to meet with them between the cherubim. In this way their need to worship would be satisfied, because God had given them a place, a structure and a system whereby they could meet with Him.

However, God's instructions guaranteed that His awesome holiness would be on everyone's mind. The ark of the covenant was to be kept in the most holy place where there was no natural light. Only the high priest was allowed to enter, and even he could enter only one day a year. Moreover, he could enter only when ceremonially cleansed, bearing first a sacrifice for his own sin and then another for the sins of all the people. The children of Israel recognized that God was present among them, but He was so other, so awesome, so removed, so distinct, so holy that they could approach Him only through their representative, and only how and when God said. This produced in them a great sense of His holiness.

It is very important to remember that the ark contained the Ten Commandments. As everybody knows, nobody has ever kept them. Not only were the tablets broken, but so too was the law. It is as we consider how mankind has broken God's law that we recognize our own sinfulness. When we look at who God is and what He expects of us, we are presented with the fact of His holiness and our sinfulness. It is significant that at the place where the high priest was to meet with God on behalf of the people, there was a constant reminder of the sinfulness of men because of the broken law. But there was also a place of atonement where sins could be forgiven. It was only on the basis of recognition of sin and of atonement for sin that they could meet with a holy God.

We must also notice that the tabernacle, and especially the ark of the covenant, were to be the focal points of life for the people of Israel. For instance, when it was time to move from one place to another in their wilderness wanderings, God would indicate this to the high priest. The other priests would collapse the coverings of the tent over the ark—they weren't allowed to see it—and then the priests would get hold of the poles fitted in the side of the ark—they couldn't touch it either. With the ark leading the way, the children of Israel would follow. In this way the forgiving God kept His promise to guide and direct His people. Even their encampment was arranged around the tabernacle. It was literally and metaphorically the center of their lives.

The ark became a source of strength and encouragement to them. After they'd wandered in the wilderness for forty years and were ready to cross the Jordan River, they were led by priests carrying the ark. As the priests stepped into the water, the Jordan ceased to flow, and they stood in the middle of the riverbed while the people walked across on dry ground. When everybody was across, the priests took the ark to the west bank and the Jordan returned to its normal course. Once again they were reminded that their God was in charge of their affairs, seeking only their loving response to His gracious care.

Turning From God's Way

As the centuries rolled by, the children of Israel became careless about worshiping as they were supposed to and slipped into nominalism and formalism. It is the easiest thing in the world to lose the reality of commitment and to simply go through the motions, until in time even the motions stop and are only periodically revived.

Fetishism—the Abuse of Worship

That's what happened to the children of Israel. On one occasion when they got into a big fight with the Philistines, they lost four thousand men on the first day of battle. In a panic the elders said, "We had better get the ark of the covenant down there."

People have all kinds of superstitions and fetishes. In the same way that soldiers in danger have a tendency to get religious—"no atheists in foxholes"—so the ancient Israelites thought that the presence of the ark on the battlefield might turn the tide, might bring them luck.

God was clearly indignant about this. He is not at all open to being used by people as a charm or a fetish, but that is what the Israelites were trying to do. He showed His indignation not only by allowing His people to be defeated, but by also allowing the ark to be captured.

Syncretism—The Confusion of Worship

The sacred ark fell into the hands of Israel's mortal enemies, the Philistines. To add insult to injury, they took the ark and put it in the temple of Dagon in the city of Ashdod. The next morning the grotesque idol, Dagon, was lying flat on his face, so they hurriedly propped him up. But the next morning he was flat on his face again. His head and hands were broken off and lying on the threshold.

God was letting them know not only that He would not be used as a fetish, but also that there was no way He would fit in with idols.

When our concepts of worship degenerate, we can get to the point where we ignore God except when we want to use Him. Other times we worship Him with the attitude, "I'll have God in this part of my life, but I'll keep my idols in the rest of it. He won't mind." This is a gross misunderstanding of the holiness of God and of what it means to worship Him in His holiness.

The Philistines decided to get the ark out of Ashdod because it was causing them nothing but trouble. So they built a cart, yoked some oxen, loaded the ark and headed it off, unsupervised, in the direction of Israel.

Imagine the surprise of those Israelites when an ox cart came trundling into their field bearing the ark of the covenant, which they had never seen or touched. The missing ark was back, but nobody particularly cared, it seems; they left it sitting in someone's barn for a long time. They were not interested in the God of the covenant or the ark. They were worshiping other gods. They would use God when they needed Him and ignore Him when they didn't want Him. They had decided that He was not their God in any real sense of the word.

Secularism—The Substitute for Worship

When David came to the throne, he led Israel in a series of victories culminating in the conquest of what we now call Jerusalem, the City of David. David recognized that Jerusalem would be the central place of worship, so he decided to bring the ark of the covenant there. No doubt his conscience was bothering him: he had built himself a magnificent palace, but the ark of the covenant was still sitting in a barn gathering dust.

David organized a party to retrieve the ark, but they made a bad mistake. They started to haul the cart with the ark on it, but one of the oxen stumbled. As the ark was about to fall off the cart, somebody grabbed it and promptly dropped dead. He was only trying to help!

But that's exactly the point. Men have to learn that they're not here to help God; they're here to do things God's way, and that is a hard lesson to learn. The children of Israel were so out of touch with God that they were emulating the Philistines instead of obeying God who had clearly stated how the ark was to be transported. God had His reasons for insisting exactly how the ark was to be handled. Those reasons were related to His holiness.

The Philistines, of course, neither knew nor cared about this, so they did what was obvious to them—they built a cart for the ark. The Israelites, on the other hand, should have known better. Maybe they were ignorant of divine principles, maybe they were just lazy, or perhaps they thought it didn't really matter. Perhaps there were some progressives in their midst who knew that in the modern world carts rather than backpacks were the way to move arks.

And today similar kinds of rationalization can lead us away from true worship into a series of activities which pass for worship but actually are little more than secular thought in ill-fitting, ecclesiastical garb. There's only one thing that will steer us away from those things and keep us on track, and that is to recognize the holiness of God, the *otherness* of God—the One before whom we come in worship.

David learned his lesson. He went back to the book and learned that the ark should be covered and carried on poles by the priests. Belatedly, he started to do things properly. It's very interesting that after the priests had gone only six steps, he told them to stop and make an offering. I suspect he was thinking, "We got it right this time! Phew! Praise the Lord!"

So David organized a whole procession to accompany the ark of the covenant to Jerusalem—a choir, a percussion group, a brass ensemble and strings—and he personally led them. He got so excited that he started singing and dancing most vigorously, and his wife Michal was not impressed. (Maybe she came from a mainline denomination!) But David was thrilled that the worship of God was finally back where it belonged. That stimulated him to encourage others to "worship the Lord in the splendor of His holiness."

But we can't leave the story of the ark just yet. After David installed the ark in its tent in Jerusalem, he wanted to build a temple for the worship of the Lord. God said this was not possible, but that David's son could build a suitable home for the ark. So Solomon built a magnificent temple, and the ark was placed in the most holy place.

Centuries later, Nebuchadnezzer and the Babylonians came, destroyed Jerusalem (including Solomon's temple), looted the holy things and carried the treasures back to Babylon.

The ark has never been seen from that day to this. Nobody knows where it is. Possibly it was destroyed. There is a legend in the Apochrypha that Jeremiah rescued it and hid it on Mount Nebo. Others say it was carried off to Babylon, and when Babylon fell, it was destroyed. Still others believe it's buried under the temple mount in Jerusalem where the Dome of the Rock now stands. That is why Orthodox Jews never walk across the temple mount for fear they might be trampling on the ark of the covenant. The ark is lost, and only Steven Spielberg and Indiana Jones thought they knew where it is!

Jesus, Our High Priest

You may be asking, "What in the world has all this history got to do with us?" Quite a lot, actually! In Hebrews 9 the story of the tabernacle and the ark is applied to the Lord Jesus. This Scripture shows how in the old days God could be approached only at the set place by the high priest bearing the blood of a sacrifice. But the Lord Jesus became our sacrifice and our High Priest. After His death and resurrection, He ascended into the presence of the most Holy God bearing the evidence of His triumphant death on our behalf.

It was no coincidence that when He died, the heavy veil which partitioned the holy of holies from the rest of the world, was torn from top to bottom, showing symbolically that a new and living way had been opened by God into His presence. This did not mean that God was no longer holy or that He was now prepared to ignore sin. On the contrary, the work of Christ on the cross underlined His holiness and His hatred of sin, and magnificently demonstrated His love and grace which accepts the repentant one and forgives the sinner.

The object of our worship is still "the Lord in His holiness," but the emphasis is on the fact that He is a holy Lord who is approachable and accessible to all in Christ. To understand the basis of our acceptance and the means of our reconciliation is to be drawn to the Lord in worship. No ark of the covenant is necessary now; in fact, it's appropriate that we don't know where it is—or even if it still exists. Nor is a high priest or a sacrificial system required, for now we have the crucified, risen Christ who makes it possible for us to come into the presence of a holy God, to acknowledge and worship Him in the splendor of His holiness. But we should not lose sight of the fact that if David could become so excited about worshiping a holy Lord in a system which was primarily symbolic, we should be capable of at least the same intensity and exuberance of worship, for we know Christ, the reality of whom the symbolism spoke.

Moreover, we need to consider the ups and downs of Israel's experience with the ark. Unless worship is approached properly, it can all too easily degenerate into nominalism, formalism, syncretism or even fetishism.

The Elements of Worship

Now assuming that we accept the premise that we are to worship, and that we understand the principles symbolized in the story of the ark, what are we supposed to do when we engage in worship? Scripture gives us three pointers in this regard.

Concentration

First of all, we need to recognize that worship requires an element of concentration. We are to worship the Lord. Our concentration is on Him. All week we have to concentrate on a thousand and one different things, but there must be times of worship, both individual and corporate, when we put other things aside and concentrate on the Lord. That is the basic point of worship.

Granted, we arrive from all points on the compass when we come into a worship experience. Some have had a great week and are rejoicing and are excited to tell their friends all about it. But some are deeply worried about family matters. Divorce papers have been served on others, and their minds and spirits are numb. Some have been to see the doctor and are waiting for the results, and can't think about anything else. Some have troubled and troublesome teenagers and are overwhelmed with a sense of failure as parents.

We come to worship with different concerns, but the uniqueness of our gathering is that we come to worship the Lord in the beauty of His holiness. This does not mean, of course, that God is disinterested in our concerns and cares. The Lord Jesus Himself said that we should weep with those who weep and rejoice with those who rejoice. But He does want us to recognize that if we come to worship but still are absorbed with our own concerns, we're really missing the point. If we focus on Him, we will get our orientation right, and we will see our concerns in a new light.

It is in the discovery and remembrance of who God is that we discover the solutions to our problems, if there are any, or the ability to live well in unsolvable problems. But the focus must be on Him, and in so doing we find the ugliness of our circumstances can be alleviated by the beauty of His holiness and the hopelessness of our situations can be contrasted with His all-surpassing grace and power.

When we concentrate on Him, we begin to focus on His glory. The psalmist said, "Declare His glory among the nations, His marvelous deeds among all peoples" (96:3). It is perfectly appropriate when we gather together in worship to recount the glory of the Lord and the wonders of what He has done. We can do this in many different ways—in our praises, in our prayers, in our testimonies and in the preaching of the Word.

Some people might say, "It's the same old stuff all the time—just recounting the same old thing." That may be true, but did you ever notice how athletes love to talk over a championship game they played years before? Have you ever heard old soldiers tell you the same war stories over and over again? And you may have indulged yourself in accounts of athletic victories of long ago that prove the truth of the adage "The older we are the better we were." We listen to them as if it's the first time we've heard them, because the storytellers enjoy the retelling. Have you been caught by a grandmother with her photographs as she told you the same cutesy things about these little rascals who turned miraculously into angels?

The same old story, if it's true, is worth repeating. Of course, it's an added bonus if the "old, old story" of the Lord can be told in a fresh way! But the recounting of who He is and what He has done will never grow stale to the worshiping heart—as long as the focus is on Him.

Consecration

As soon as our concentration is on the Lord, we are face-to-face with His awesomeness, His otherness, His holiness, which leads us to recognize that in comparison to Him and His wonders, the things that clutter our lives are relatively insignificant. Despite that, they may have become our idols. David reminded the people, "Great is the Lord and most worthy of praise; He is to be feared above all gods. For all the gods of the nations are idols, but the Lord made the heavens" (1 Chron. 16:25–26).

The contrast here is incredible. The gods of the nations are literally nothing, but the Lord made the heavens. Concentration on who the Lord is can lead to the discovery that things which are so significant to me are "nothings" compared to Him. I begin to see again that my orientation and my perspective and my sense of values are all wrong, and I come before Him with a sense of His holiness. I turn away from the "idols" and revere Him afresh in all the wonder of His person. This tremendous sense of reverence is stressed in David's psalm: "He is to be feared above all gods. . . . Tremble before Him, all the earth!" (1 Chron. 16:25, 30).

We come into the presence of the living God for corporate worship very conscious of who it is that we're meeting, and we conduct ourselves and our affairs as consecrated people. The Hebrew word for worship means "to bow down." In the Greek one of the words for worship means "to kiss toward." It is an act of submission, like a servant honoring a master.

The correct attitude of worship is to come before the Lord focusing on Him, His glory, His marvelous deeds, what He has done in our lives, recognizing His awesomeness and our sinfulness, glorying in the fact that Christ alone is our great High Priest who has provided access into the presence of a holy God. We come humbly, devotedly, committed to Him as consecrated people. That is worship.

Celebration

There should be a strong element of celebration in worship, but not at the expense of reverence. Some people are into reverence, and some people are into celebration, but not everybody is into both! You have probably heard some of the arguments about the appropriate way to worship. You may even have been unfortunate enough to be caught in the middle of one of them! The big question is, "Should worship be a solemn convocation, or should it be a joyful celebration?" And the answer, of course, is yes. It should be both.

But how? David managed it. He talked about fearing the Lord and trembling before Him, but at the same time he came into the place of worship, took off his royal robes and led the procession in singing and dancing! No doubt when the people saw His Majesty doing this, they joined right in, and before you know it they were having a joy-filled celebration! The question is, "Is it appropriate for us to celebrate joyously in worship?" David thought so. In First Chronicles 16 he said,

Sing to the Lord, all the earth (16:23).

Let the heavens rejoice, let the earth be glad (16:31).

Let the sea resound (16:32).

Let the fields be jubilant (16:32).

The trees of the forest will sing, they will sing for joy before the Lord (16:33).

Praise be to the Lord (16:36).

Then all the people said, "Amen" and "Praise the Lord" (16:36).

But how can we both celebrate and be solemn? We can do both when we come before His presence recognizing the awesomeness of His person and the awfulness of our condition, but remembering that Christ, our great High Priest, has opened a new and a living way to the Father. He welcomes us into His presence, and the welcome makes us rejoice; the sense of His presence keeps it within bounds.

John Wesley loved to sing God's praises. He rode on horseback tens of thousands of miles, studying his Greek New Testament as he went with the reins thrown over the horse's neck. (Presumably the horse knew where the next preaching engagement was!) Then he would put his Testament in a saddlebag, lift his hands to heaven and start singing at the top of his voice as he rode through the valleys and the dales and the forests of England.

It is not surprising, therefore, that when the Wesleyan revival came along, he and his brother Charles taught the people to sing, and told them, "Sing at your work." Why was that? Because when you understand the wonder of your salvation, your heart is filled with inexpressible joy all day, every day, and singing is one of the greatest ways to express it. So learn to celebrate in worship and make sure you sing!

You may say, "I don't like singing." Well, I've got some sad news for you—you'll be miserable for all eternity if you don't like singing. Start practicing now! In a hurry! You may say, "I don't have a voice." Sure you do. It may not be a good one, but it can make a joyful noise. So sing in celebration!

We also share with others in celebration. We are to "declare His glory among the nations" (1 Chron. 16:24). Telling people about the glorious deeds of the Lord is not easy. Timidity, fear of rejection, inadequate grasp of the subject—all these tend to affect us. Nevertheless, if we worship the Lord in the beauty of His holiness and discover the wonder of His person all over again, the desire to help others discover what we have found will outweigh the intimidating factors.

We celebrate by sacrificing too. The instructions are quite straightforward. "Bring an offering and come before Him; worship the Lord in the splendor of His holiness" (1 Chron. 16:29).

Bring some tangible evidence that you love the Lord, something that is the product of your labor, that is therefore part of you, and then rejoice as you give sacrificially to Him and His cause in gratitude. Let me close with four very simple suggestions:

1. Regard worship as a priority to be established.

2. Regard worship as a privilege to be appreciated.

3. Regard worship as a pleasure to be enjoyed.

4. Regard worship as a practice to be developed.

Worship the Lord in the beauty of holiness!

PRAYER

Lord, we have endeavored to focus our attention upon You. We've endeavored to lay aside our cares and concerns, and gaze upon You, to think of Your glory and Your wonderful works. We ask that Your Spirit would help us to respond appropriately, for we pray in Christ's name. Amen.

A PERSONAL NOTE FROM JILL

One day in my devotional time, I read the story of King David and Absalom (2 Sam. 13–15). Absalom had rebelled against his father. What a betrayal—what shock and chagrin David must have experienced!

After the incident was over, David was restored to his throne. He then had to deal with a beloved but rebellious child. He allowed Absalom to live in the same city but banished him from his personal presence. In the words of Scripture, he was "not allowed to see the king's face."

This went on for three years until Absalom could bear it no longer and protested vigorously. David relented, forgave him, and fellowship was restored.

I thought about the immediate personal application of this incident. I recognized it was possible to live within close proximity of the King and yet somehow never see His face. That's like attending a church service but never catching a glimpse of God—a common thing that can lead to spiritual disappointment and discouragement.

I was amazed that this could go on for three years, and yet I knew in my own case months can go by without contact with the King. I wondered if Absalom attended worship through this period, hoping for a glimpse of David. Did he leave time after time bitterly disappointed and discouraged?

In the end Absalom verbalized his frustration about the situation and took steps to put it right. Like David's son, I knew that because of the mercy seat and the atonement that Jesus had accomplished for me, all I needed to do was verbalize my unhappiness about the situation too. Then I needed to take steps to put things right—leave my sin behind me, promise to be obedient and throw myself on His grace.

Like father and child in the story, I took these steps. I found forgiveness and I saw my Father's face.

It struck me that David was as unhappy as Absalom about the invisible wall between them. It had certainly been right and necessary to punish Absalom for his rebellion. But David loved his son and was overjoyed when a personal touch was restored.

When I think of worship, I personally need to remember my side and God's side. He can bring blessing and a song to my heart, and I can bring pleasure to His.

Unfortunately, events show Absalom did not continue in unbroken fellowship and service with David. He broke faith with the command of the king. The glorious day that David and Absalom reconciled was brief—too brief. It is a reminder that true worship is a moment-by-moment matter. It is far more than rituals in the temple—it is a moment-by-moment attitude, a walking in the holy light and with the holy King of kings and Lord of lords.

Oh, that I may truly grieve over any little disobedience that may make of me an Absalom, thereby bringing great grief to my Father's heart.

CHAPTER QUESTIONS

1. God gave the children of Israel specific instructions concerning a worship center. The ark of the covenant, in which lay the Ten Commandments which the people had broken, was in the holy of holies, the only place God would meet with His people.

    a. What does this say to you? What should be at the heart of our worship?

    b. The loving obedience of the children of Israel was to be demonstrated in worship. It follows that to be disobedient in this regard is sin. What does this say to you?

    c. The idea of meeting God in a holy place in the presence of the ark which held the Ten Commandments is a powerful thought. How does this equate with your Sunday worship experience?

2. As the children of Israel moved, they carried the ark with them. So often when we move either from childhood to adulthood, from one location to another, or for other reasons, we leave the "ark" behind us, as corporate worship ceases to be a priority. True worship, however, demands that God and His Word be the focal point of our lives as it was for the Israelites. If you can sincerely do so, fill in your personal promises below:

    a. I will recommit my life to the worship and service of God.
    Signature _____

    b. I will meet with Him regularly.
    Time: Mon.–Fri._____ Sat._____ Sun._____

    c. I will begin to systematically read a portion of Scripture regularly, starting with _____.
                          (Book of the Bible)

    d. Knowing I need to be alone, I will do this in/at
    _____.
               (place)

    e. I will involve myself in a fellowship of believers in corporate worship at _____.
                      (where)

3. Write a sentence definition of the following:

    a. Fetishism

    b. Syncretism

    c. Secularism

4. Read Hebrews 9. Presuming you are already trying to worship God, what necessary element needs your personal effort at this time?

   a. Concentration

   b. Consecration

   c. Celebration

5. Write a few lines about one new thing you have learned from this study or something you knew already but needed to be reminded of at this time.

10

&

The Holy City

Then I saw a new heaven and a new earth, for the first heaven and the first earth had passed away, and there was no longer any sea. I saw the Holy City, the new Jerusalem, coming down out of heaven from God, prepared as a bride beautifully dressed for her husband. And I heard a loud voice from the throne saying, "Now the dwelling of God is with men, and He will live with them. They will be His people, and God Himself will be with them and be their God. He will wipe every tear from their eyes. There will be no more death or mourning or crying or pain, for the old order of things has passed away." (Rev. 21:1–4)

The Book of Revelation is an account of a series of visions given by God to the apostle John, who was the overseer of the church at Ephesus. He had gotten into trouble with the authorities and had been exiled to the Isle of Patmos. The visions were recorded in a literary genre called apocalyptic—a style of writing common in antiquity but practically unknown today. Apocalyptic literature utilized a considerable amount of symbolism—numbers, earthquakes, dragons and assorted grotesque beasts. Readers of this literature had to use interpretive skills to understand what was being communicated.

Provided the readers and author were on the same wavelength, interpretation posed no problem; but if this were not the case, there were very real communication problems. This was both good and bad. It was good, if like John, you wanted to say some rude things about the authorities (with whom you were already in trouble) without their realizing what you were saying! It was bad if, like us, you are trying to understand the literature almost two thousand years after it was penned, living as we do in a cultural milieu far removed from that of which John and his readers were a part.

If, however, we believe that inspired Scripture is relevant today as well as appropriate to the age in which it was written, we can and must approach passages such as the one before us humbly, carefully and expectantly.

This particular passage of Scripture talks about the Holy City. This is of particular interest to us, since no study on holiness can be complete without an understanding of the Holy City. So while John's vision is full of exciting and puzzling symbolism, we can confidently ask that God by His Spirit will help us to understand and apply what the Spirit said, and is still saying, to the churches.

A Vision of Deity

After the disintegration of the Soviet Union—the public discrediting of Marxist Leninism, the mad scramble to independence by the former Soviet Republics, the heady emancipation of the former satellite states of Eastern Europe—the Western world breathed a collective sigh of relief. The Berlin Wall came "a-tumblin' down," nuclear submarines stayed in port, and vines grew up over silos containing hideous weapons of mass destruction. The President of the United States proclaimed "a new world order," and the hope which springs eternal in the human breast sprang!

Unfortunately, the euphoria which greeted the advent of this new world order was shaken by Saddam Hussein, his ill-fated excursion into Kuwait and the resultant blowup in the Middle East. That was dealt with, more or less, for a while, and now years later, while Saddam Hussein has long departed this scene, the region he ruled is far from settled.

When Marshal Tito was no more, Yugoslavia erupted, genocide reared its vicious head and the Balkans erupted and disintegrated, but at present an uneasy calm prevails. And Afghanistan is proving once again what we have always suspected—it is intractable.

As I write from the Middle East, Libya has been torn apart by civil war; Egypt has experienced revolution, and it is anyone's guess as to where it goes from here. Bahrain is troubled, Saudi Arabia is perturbed, Iran is exacerbating, Yemen is in ferment, and Israel is watching carefully.

All of this leads us to wonder whatever happened to this "new world order."

This is not to decry noble efforts to bring peace, nor is it to suggest that we should not be desperately concerned and committed to working to this end. The desire for a new world order indicates an appropriate disillusionment with the status quo and a desire for something better. The question is, Can we hope for anything better than a new world order of human manufacture, which produces little that is new and even less in the way of world order?

God has not promised a new world order *per se*, but He is committed to creating, eventually and finally, a new heaven and a new earth, including the Holy City that is grander and greater than human beings have ever imagined or could ever create.

The vision of the Holy City opens with God sitting on the throne. The best way to understand anything is to start with a vision of Deity, which incorporates a vision of eternity. Notice that in the book of Revelation God is seated on a throne. That is His normal posture. This speaks of His sovereignty. It insists that He is ultimately in control of all things. In very graphic terms John said, "I saw a great white throne and Him who was seated on it. Earth and sky fled from His presence, and there was no place for them" (20:11). In other words, he saw an awesome God, high and holy, transcending all things, ruling the universe.

Now some people don't accept that there is a sovereign God working out His purposes in the world. As far as I can see, the alternatives are either that mankind is in charge of our world (in which case the appropriate prayer would be, "God help us!") or that everything is up for grabs and blind chance rules. Which would you prefer? Blind chance? Fallible man? Or sovereign God? Whose finger would you prefer on the button? The Bible unequivocally states that the Lord is sovereign and that it is He who speaks to John.

God prefaced His statement to John with "These words are trustworthy and true." He is ready to talk about the end of the world and what happens afterward, a subject of great fascination and speculation among humans, and one in which imagination can blossom. But the end of the world and what comes after that are not subjects for idle speculation; they require divine revelation. Therefore, it is reassuring to hear, "These words are trustworthy and true." And it is worth noting that He also wanted these words carefully recorded—"Write this down" (Rev. 21:5)—presumably in order that they might be preserved and read at a later time.

As if to state His credentials to speak authoritatively, God said, "I am the Alpha and the Omega, the Beginning and the End" (Rev. 21:6). *Alpha* is the first letter of the Greek alphabet and *Omega* is the final letter. In modern parlance, we talk about knowing a subject "from A to Z." That is the English equivalent of "Alpha to Omega." God is the One who knows the whole story—the meta-narrative!

Greek letters were also used numerically so that *Alpha* was 1, *Beta* was 2, *Gamma* was 3, *Delta* was 4, and so on. If God is the Alpha, He is also Number One! Sports fans shout loud and long about various football teams being number one. Perhaps it is time for a renewed proclamation that He who is seated on the throne is Alpha, Number One. He is also Omega, for He goes right to the end. He is the sum totality of all things.

He is the beginning and He is the ending. When we think in terms of human history, we automatically think about where it began, and we ponder about where it will end. Whenever origins are discussed, the word evolution inevitably appears. G.K. Chesterton wrote:

> Most modern histories of mankind begin with the word evolution. As a matter of fact it is not, touching these primary things, a very practical word or a very profitable idea. Nobody can imagine how nothing could turn into something. Nobody can get an inch nearer to it by explaining how something could turn into something else. It is really far more logical to start by saying, "In the beginning God created heaven and earth," even if you only mean, "In the beginning some unthinkable power began some unthinkable process."[15]

If we want to talk about origins, evolution doesn't help. The best that evolution can do is offer explanations of how something turned into something else. But that has nothing to do with origins. *Origins* addresses the mystery of how something which wasn't, now is! How did nothing become something? Evolution may well be an explanation of human development, but that is all.

Any adequate explanation of human origins must address the mystery of how there was something or someone independent enough and powerful enough to make nothing into something. The divine title *Alpha,* or "beginning," addresses the issue and makes a clear statement concerning humanity's divine origins.

The Greek word *Telos* means "end," "goal" or "objective." To understand where human history is going, we need to recognize that it doesn't simply repeat itself; neither is it going to fizzle into a cosmic whimper or self-destruct in a cosmic explosion. The Bible teaches that human history is working toward an end, a goal, an objective, and it's all found in God. In fact, He is the end!

A Vision of Eternity

John's vision of Deity included a vision of eternity. In the vision, "Alpha and Omega, the beginning and the end," having insisted that He is "faithful and true," spoke from His throne, the seat of ultimate control, and said, "I am making everything new. . . . The old order of things has passed away" (Rev. 21:5). Before we look into the language used to describe the "everything new" of which God spoke, let me remind you about the "old order of things" which God declares "has passed away."

The Bible begins with a powerful and fundamental statement: "In the beginning God created the heavens and the earth." Nobody can prove it or disprove it. You either accept it or reject it. It is a matter of faith either way—you either believe that God is, or you believe that God isn't.

Understandings of origins flow from that initial faith position. God, according to the biblical account, gave His creation straight A's. "Very good," He said. "Very good, very good, very good!" The pinnacle of the created order was humanity made in the image of God with the incredible capability of knowing God, loving God, obeying God, honoring God, serving God and bringing glory to God.

In order for that to happen, God sovereignly decided that mankind should be vested with a remarkable capability called free will. Now free will doesn't mean anything unless there are options, which God gave. Option One was, "Obey Me, honor Me, love Me, and you will live." Option Two was, "Disobey Me, dishonor Me, rebel against Me, and you will die." It was all very clearly explained. Option Two was the one Adam and Eve chose, and the result was a cataclysmic fall. People were estranged from God, society started to fragment, and the whole creation was corrupted and began to suffer and groan. That's the way it is right now, but things will not stay like this.

Interestingly, I have discovered all over the world a basic point of agreement. "Things are not the way they ought to be." People agree with this and are eager to give examples. But what they often overlook is the simple fact that if "things are not the way they ought to be" that assumes there is a way they ought to be. And the difference between what is and what should be is called "The Fall." And it is in evidence wherever you look.

The Bible tells us that "the day of the Lord will come" (2 Pet. 3:10), when God determines that the world will come to an end. God, having created and sustained it, will bring it to an appointed end. God, who initiated and perpetuated, is the One who ultimately will terminate His creation. "The heavens will disappear with a roar; the elements will be destroyed by fire, and the earth and everything in it will be laid bare," Peter warned (3:10). But he added that God will make "a new heaven and a new earth, the home of righteousness" (3:13). This is the vision of the future that Scripture clearly enunciates. This new heaven and new earth created by God will incorporate a city called the New Jerusalem.

The New Jerusalem/the Old Jerusalem

In his vision, John saw coming out of heaven a city with very unusual dimensions. He measured it and found it was 12,000 stadia by 12,000 stadia by 12,000 stadia—a 1,500-mile cubic city suspended in midair. What is important about this vision is the grandeur and the immensity of what will come from the Lord's hand. The New Jerusalem is a divine creation.

Before we think more about the New Jerusalem, let us refresh our minds concerning the old Jerusalem. In the Psalms Jerusalem was called "the place where God's glory dwells." But the prophet Ezekiel recorded the departure of the glory of God from the Holy City. Reluctantly, the *Shekinah* glory left the most holy place, moved to the threshold of the temple, then to the Eastern Gate; and then, after lingering over the Mount of Olives, the visible evidence of God's glory (presence) departed from Jerusalem.

When Jesus spent time in Jerusalem and saw what was going on there, He burst into tears and said, "O Jerusalem, Jerusalem . . . how often I have longed to gather your children together, as a hen gathers her chicks under her wings, but you were not willing" (Matt. 23:37). The glory of the Lord had departed from the earthly Jerusalem because the people had rebelled against their God and resisted His loving attempts to gather them to Himself and protect them from themselves. They had constantly stoned and killed the prophets whom God had sent to them, and in the end they had screamed for the crucifixion of the King of Glory on a hill outside Jerusalem's wall. Far from being the place where God dwelt in glory, Jerusalem had fallen into deep shame.

But God had not finally deserted His chosen city. In the same way that the old heavens and the old earth had become so corrupted that they must of necessity be terminated, and a new heaven and a new earth created, so the old Jerusalem, now figuratively called Sodom and Egypt in Revelation 11:8, would be terminated, and a New Jerusalem would take its place.

A Tale of Two Cities

The glory of the New Jerusalem was accentuated in John's vision by setting it in marked contrast to another city, Babylon. In fact, a case could be made for calling the Book of Revelation "A Tale of Two Cities"—Babylon and Jerusalem. In Revelation the great city Babylon epitomizes everything that is sordid about our world. This present world order is like Babylon shot through with corruption, and it will come to an end. In its place will be created a new city characterized by righteousness. It will be "the dwelling of God" (Rev. 21:3) and will shine with "the glory of God" (Rev. 21:11). Its focal point will be "the throne of God."

The end of the old Jerusalem which had become part of Babylon, and the creation of the New Jerusalem characterized by God gloriously present in her midst, ruling and reigning in righteousness, was the content of John's vision. In dramatic language he announced that because the glory of God will pervade the Holy City, there will be no need for the sun or the moon. There will not be any sea, and there will not be any night there. There will be no more pain, and there will not be any death, and every last tear will be personally wiped away by God Himself!

Isn't that what people are looking for? Isn't that the dream for which mankind is searching vainly in a new world order? Isn't that the hope which springs eternal in the human breast? This is precisely what God has promised. He who sits on the throne, the Alpha and the Omega, the Beginning and the End, has announced that He will bring the old order to an end and make everything new.

The Wife of the Lamb

When I was in school, my English teacher used to warn me against split infinitives and mixed metaphors. As an example of the latter she would recite, with great glee, an excerpt from the speech of a member of Parliament. The right honorable member had said, "I smell a rat, I see it floating in the air, I'll nip it in the bud!" His metaphors were not only mixed—they were mercilessly mangled!

John did not worry about mixed metaphors either. Probably it was impossible to be an apocalyptic writer and not mix them! Note how he not only talked about the New Jerusalem as the Holy City but also identified it as "the bride, the wife of the Lamb" (Rev. 21:9). What did he mean? Who is the Lamb? And who or what is His bride?

The Lamb figures largely in the Book of Revelation. In the early part of his vision, John was deeply troubled that no one in creation was found worthy to "open the scroll or look inside" (Rev. 5:4), or to unravel the mysteries of God's universe and unveil His eternal purposes. He was told, however, that "the Lion of the tribe of Judah" (Rev 5:5) was both willing and able to do it and that John could meet Him! Amazingly, the Lion appeared as a Lamb "looking as if it had been slain, standing in the center of the throne" (Rev. 5:6). Whoever heard of a dead lamb standing up? Well, when Jesus started His ministry, John the Baptist introduced Him as "the Lamb of God" (John 1:36), and the apostle Paul picked up on the idea and called the Lord Jesus "our Passover Lamb" (1 Cor. 5:7).

In the same way that at the original Passover in Egypt the Pascal Lamb had been killed to provide redemption, so Jesus died and rose again to provide redemption for mankind. He is the dead Lamb standing up!

Who or what is "the bride, the wife of the Lamb"? The Holy City. In Ephesians 5 Paul used the marital relationship as an analogy of the relationship between Christ and His church. There's the key. The church is the bride of the Lamb. This is made quite clear in Revelation 19:7–8:

> "For the wedding of the Lamb has come,
> > and His bride has made herself ready.
> Fine linen, bright and clean,
> > was given her to wear."
> (Fine linen stands for the righteous acts of the saints.)

Who are the saints? They are the holy ones set apart to God for His service. What is the Holy City, the New Jerusalem, the bride, the wife of the Lamb? What is this new creation of God that will take the place of the old Jerusalem that denied her God? She is the company of the redeemed, those who have acknowledged Jesus as their crucified, risen and glorified Lord, and have taken their stand as His saints, His holy ones, set apart for His service.

What is going to happen in the future? The Alpha and the Omega, the Beginning and the End, who obviously ought to know, has said that He will bring about the end of the present world order and put in its place everything new, including the Holy City, the bride comprised of those who love the risen Christ. God has drawn the drapes on eternity just a little to let us peek inside.

The Dark Side

There is a dark side to this vision which must not be ignored. Sitting on His throne, the Lord told John, "The cowardly, the unbelieving, the vile, the murderers, the sexually immoral, those who practice magic arts, the idolaters and all liars—their place will be in the fiery lake of burning sulphur. This is the second death" (Rev. 21:8). Deep down most believers wish that this were not the case, and that they could adhere to a universalistic theology, which means that everything will come out all right in the wash, and that everybody will finish up in heaven.

However, Scripture gives no basis for such a belief. Unrepentant sinners could not be in God's presence for all eternity. They could not stand it, and His holiness could not permit it. It might appear gracious of God to allow the unrepentant into the Holy City, but it would not be righteous. The unrepentant might be blessed, but their human uniqueness would have been debased and destroyed. The nature of both God and mankind requires alternate destinies. Principles of human existence ordained from the beginning, allowing choice and options, blessing and cursing, require ultimate conclusions—time's experiences projected into eternal finality.

The vision of eternity shows those who have acknowledged Christ as Savior and Lord constituting His Bride, the Holy City, and those who did not, experiencing the second death. If the first death means, among other things, separation from loved ones, the second death means separation from God. This is described in dramatic, awesome terms because simple human language could not adequately portray the difference between being a member of the Holy City and being a member of the lost community. Those are the eternal options.

A Vision of Humanity

If this is what is going to happen in the eternal future, what kind of concern should believers have for those we know and love, in order that they might rightly understand eternal issues? There is much ignorance and wishful thinking when it comes to eternal destiny, but Scripture is excruciatingly blunt: "Nothing impure will ever enter it [the Holy City], nor will anyone who does what is shameful or deceitful" (Rev. 21:27).

So much for people who assume that they will walk into glory on the basis of some self-evaluated and ill-defined "good life." The word from the throne is that citizenship in the Holy City is reserved for "those whose names are written in the Lamb's Book of Life" (Rev. 21:27).

Entrance to the Holy City is free, the price of admission having already been paid. We call it redemption. Those who have received the gift of eternal life from the Lamb of God once slain and now risen anticipate living eternally with Him. Another way of looking at it is found in God's offer: "To him who is thirsty I will give to drink without cost from the spring of the water of life" (Rev. 21:6). Those who thirst for spiritual and eternal life can come to God. It is available to them, purchased by Christ and freely offered.

So who are those who will constitute the Holy City? Those whose names are written in the Lamb's Book of Life, because they were thirsty enough for spiritual things to come to God through Christ and freely drink of Him. Those who overcome and persist in their faith. They will keep on keeping on. This is the glorious prospect that God presents to men and women today.

The alternative? "If anyone's name was not found written in the Book of Life, he was thrown into the lake of fire" (Rev. 20:15). "Hellfire and brimstone" are not politically correct or socially acceptable terms today. It must be admitted that some preaching of this type has been guilty of overly dramatic application coupled with flamboyant oratory. Practitioners of this style of preaching have been satirized and criticized as uncaring, insensitive, anachronistic bullies.

It may well be that their excessive, speculative dwelling on the heat of the flames or the smell of the brimstone has done less than justice to the symbolic nature of the biblical data. But excesses on this side are certainly no more to be desired than excessive neglect or ridicule of principles clearly enunciated concerning the awfulness of lostness.

If there is a heaven to be gained, there is a hell to be shunned. To deny or ignore either is to be unfaithful to Scripture and unfair to people. Let us be careful to confront the awesomeness of these truths. Those whose names are in the Lamb's Book of Life will be given free admission into the Holy City, and those who are not will be given free admission into a lost eternity.

The Holy City and Holiness

You may be wondering, "What does the Holy City have to do with holiness?" Everything! If we're heading for a Holy City, clearly holiness is our end. If holiness is our ultimate aim and our foreordained goal, then holiness must be the dominant theme of our lives on our journey. Why would anybody who wants to live in the Holy City not be interested in practicing holiness on the way? And why would anyone who now prefers the "unholy city" imagine they would enjoy the Holy City for eternity? They'd hate it!

And there's another consideration. If it is true that people are heading for an eternity either in the Holy City or in separation from God, would it not be reasonable to assume that those who are set apart for God's service would carry a heavy burden, a deep concern, about where people will spend eternity? Of course they would!

I frequently hear earnest church people ask, "Why are we considering reaching more people when we've got so many hurting people already in the fellowship? And why with so much need on our doorstep are we spending money and manpower overseas?" The church certainly has no shortage of hurting people, and they need to be cared for, but there are infinitely more perishing people outside the fellowship than there are hurting people inside. If we must choose between helping the hurting and saving the perishing, the choice is obvious.

Fortunately, we don't have to choose. It's not an either/or proposition but a both/and. We need to bring healing to the hurting, by making sure that there's plenty of discipleship and worship and fellowship available to them; these are the spiritual therapeutics which the hurting ones so desperately need.

I fully recognize that the intensity of emotional pain suffered by many is so all-consuming that until a measure of healing is achieved, there is little likelihood of them recognizing the condition of others, let alone addressing it. But let us also gently remind the hurting that sometimes the best therapy for them is to devote themselves to reaching perishing people, and in their pain to recognize the even worse condition of others. "I grumbled," says the proverb, "when I had no shoes, until I saw a man who had no feet." Shoelessness, bad as it is, loses some of its pain in the company of footlessness—and loses even more of its pain when endeavoring to alleviate the suffering experienced by the footless.

The large numbers of church attenders who are along for the ride must also be stirred to an appreciation of the destiny of those not bound for the Holy City. They need to seriously evaluate their own spiritual condition and that of those with whom they rub shoulders on a daily basis who are eternity-bound.

In Conclusion

How should we wrap up our exploration of holiness? We began by looking back an eternity to the Holy One and concluded by looking eternally forward to the Holy City. Clearly, there is a golden theme of holiness running throughout Scripture that originates in the nature of God and dominates His purposes. It reaches out to mankind, touching and renewing spiritually and ethically, relationally and eternally. It must not be ignored, for it cries out to be heard. Pulpits must proclaim it, pews must embrace it. The human condition is related to it, for our destiny is wrapped up in it. The way we live now is governed by it, and the where of our eternal residence is bound to it. So the knowledge of the Holy One being understanding, let us leave no stone unturned in our pursuit of knowing Him and applying what we know.

A Personal Meditation

Have I come to Christ, gladly acknowledging Him as my Savior and Lord, receiving from Him the gift of eternal life? Do I believe my name is on record in the Lamb's Book of Life? If so, I'm on my way to the Holy City. As I journey, am I living a holy life, fit for the Master's use?

PRAYER

O Lord, by Your Spirit impress these things upon my heart and help me in the intimacy of my relationship with You to get things squared away, so that it may be obvious to all who observe my daily life that I have an ongoing commitment to holiness. In Christ's name, Amen.

A PERSONAL NOTE FROM JILL

Heaven has always played a big part in my earthly pilgrimage of faith. As a child of World War II, I heard of hundreds of people daily being pitched into eternity! I wondered what it was like to die and find yourself in a better place. To my small mind the stars looked like holes in heaven with the glory shining through, a happy contrast to an adult's dark night of trouble in a frightening world.

Unchurched, yet with believing parents, I heard a little about the happy land above the worlds—heaven—and I liked what I heard. It brought a measure of security to my extremely insecure environment. Later came my conversion at the age of eighteen. In the words of a song:

Heaven came down and glory filled my soul,
When at the cross the Savior made me whole.
My sins were washed away and my night was turned to day,
Heaven came down and glory filled my soul![16]

Now I began to know that Jesus was heaven itself, and yet there was more. One day I would know perfectly what now I could only know imperfectly. Now I looked through a dark glass, but then I would see Him face to face.

Yet coming to Christ gave me a set of biblical facts that changed the entire direction of my life. For the first time I now believed there was an alternative to heaven—hell. Being able to believe everyone would get to heaven in the end, whatever sort of life they had lived, had left me free to indulge myself in a thoroughly self-centered lifestyle. Now it was totally different.

I learned from Revelation how incredible heaven was going to be and how beyond grim description would be the lot of the lost. How could I then do anything else with my life than work my head off until those I loved were safely traveling alongside me in the right direction? These convictions affected everything: my career choice, the use of my time, talents, money—even the choice of a marriage partner. To me the only feasible option in this regard was to marry a man who shared my deep spiritual concerns and was totally abandoned to the purposes of God.

Now, some fifty-five years after my conversion experience, my deep desire to see people enter the kingdom of heaven through the narrow gate that leads to life, rather than to continue on the broad road that leads to destruction, burns within me as fiercely as ever. Being in the autumn years of my life, I am aware that I grow nearer to heaven every day! Now I need to consider what is the most strategic use of my remaining years.

The theology of heaven works itself into my daily thinking, my choices and actions, my plans and dreams, my disciplines and lifestyle, and above all else it makes me ready to give an answer to anyone who asks me about the hope of heaven that I have.

Years ago, with our children grown and gone, we sold our family home and moved into a condominium. The day came when the carpet salesman arrived and tried to sell me the thickest and most expensive of his wares.

"Tell me about the other carpets," I asked him, when I could get a word in edgewise.

"Well," he said reluctantly, "this quality will last you ten years and this one twenty. But the one I think you should buy will last forty years!" I was flattered. I must have looked my best that morning! However, I chose the twenty-year quality, explaining to the startled man that this would bring me to my allotted span, three-score years and ten, and would probably be all I would need. As his mouth fell open, I took advantage of his surprise and told him a little about heaven and Jesus! I trust he thought about my words.

We need to redeem the time for the days are evil. We need to renew our vows to God and be busy in evangelism.

Above all, we need to remember that the greatest argument for the gospel is to live a holy life. We must press on to this end!

CHAPTER QUESTIONS

1. "God has promised a new world order—a new heaven and earth, including the Holy City, which is grander and greater than human beings have ever imagined or could ever create."

a. To help us "see" what John saw, look up these other references to like experiences in the Scriptures.
   What did John see? (Rev. 1:12–17)
   What did Daniel see? (Dan. 7:9–28)
   What did Isaiah see? (Isa. 6:1–8)
   What did Ezekiel see? (Ezek. 1:25–28)

b. Make a list of common elements in all of these visions.

c. What was the common reaction of all these men on seeing the vision?

d. What does this say to you?

e. Spend time worshiping God for what you have "seen" as you have read these word pictures.

2. Read Revelation 21:1–2 and Revelation 22:3. The Holy City, the New Jerusalem, is identified as the Bride of the Lamb—the church in Revelation 19:6–8.

a. Is this a new thought to you?

b. What excites you about this?

c. What scares you?

d. What challenges you?

3. In light of this study, write a paragraph that speaks of your concern for unbelievers.

a. Make a list of those you will diligently pray for.

b. Be quiet before God and think of one way you could become the answer to your own prayer. This involvement cannot be accomplished without a personal commitment to holiness.

ENDNOTES

1. Michael Green, *Evangelism through the Local Church* (London: Hodder and Stoughton, 1990), 214.
2. Frederick W. Faber, "My God, How Wonderful Thou Art" (hymn), public domain.
3. Diogenes Allen, *Christian Belief in a Post-Modern World* (Louisville: Westminster/John Knox Press, 1989), 46.
4. Ibid.
5. Elizabeth Barrett Browning, *Aurora Leigh* (epic poem), public domain.
6. F.F. Bruce, *The Book of Acts* (Grand Rapids: Eerdmans, 1954), 351.
7. Bishop William Frey of the Trinity Episcopal School for Ministry, as quoted in *Time*, June 24, 1991.
8. John White, *The Fight* (Downers Grove, IL: InterVarsity Press, 1976), 179.
9. Ibid., 180.
10. Thomas C. Oden, *After Modernity—What?* (Grand Rapids: Zondervan, 1990), 39.
11. Guy King, *II Timothy—To My Son: An Expositional Study* (Fort Washington, PA: CLC Publications, 2005 [1944, 1971]), 187.
12. These statistics and others have been compiled by pollsters such as Gallup and Barna, and are freely quoted by many authors, such as Stephen Prothero, *Religious Lit-*

eracy: What Every American Needs to Know—and Doesn't
(New York: HarperCollins, 2008).

13.   John Newton, "Come, My Soul, Thy Suit Prepare"
      (hymn), public domain.

14.   R.C. Trench, as quoted by William Barclay, The New Daily Study Bible: The Letters to Timothy, Titus and Philemon
      (Louisville, KY: Westminster John Knox Press, 2003), 69.

15.   G.K. Chesterton, The Everlasting Man (New York: Doubleday Image Books, 1955), 24–25.

16.   John W. Peterson, "Heaven Came Down and Glory Filled My Soul" (song), copyright 1961.

This book was produced by CLC Publications. We hope it has been life-changing and has given you a fresh experience of God through the work of the Holy Spirit. CLC Publications is an outreach of CLC Ministries International, a global literature mission with work in over fifty countries. If you would like to know more about us or are interested in opportunities to serve with a faith mission, we invite you to contact us at:

CLC Ministries International
PO Box 1449
Fort Washington, PA 19034

Phone: 215-542-1242
E-mail: orders@clcpublications.com
Website: www.clcpublications.com

DO YOU LOVE GOOD CHRISTIAN BOOKS?
Do you have a heart for worldwide missions?

You can receive a FREE subscription to
CLC's newsletter on global literature missions
Order by e-mail at:

clcworld@clcusa.org

Or fill in the coupon below and mail to:

**PO Box 1449
Fort Washington, PA 19034**

FREE *CLC WORLD* SUBSCRIPTION!

Name: _____

Address:_____

_____

Phone: _____ E-mail:_____

READ THE REMARKABLE STORY OF
the founding of
CLC INTERNATIONAL

Leap of Faith

"Any who doubt that Elijah's God still lives ought to read of the money supplied when needed, the stores and houses provided, and the appearance of personnel in answer to prayer." —Moody Monthly

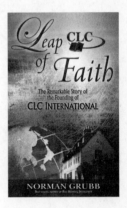

Is it possible that the printing press, the editor's desk, the Christian bookstore and the mail order department can glow with the fast-moving drama of an "Acts of the Apostles"?

Find the answer as you are carried from two people in an upstairs bookroom to a worldwide chain of Christian bookcenters multiplied by nothing but a "shoestring" of faith and by committed, though unlikely, lives.

To order your copy of *Leap of Faith*

You may order by:
Phone: 1-215-542-1240
E-mail: orders@clcpublications.com
Mail: PO Box 1449
Fort Washington, PA 19034

Discount Code: LoF 650
Reg. Price: ~~$11.99~~
Special Mission Price: $5.40
Shipping in US: $4.00
You pay: $9.40

Name: _____

Address:_____

_____

Phone: _____ E-mail: _____

DAILY THOUGHTS ON HOLINESS

Andrew Murray

A spiritual treasure trove from a veteran of the faith

Whether you have been blessed for years by the ministry of Andrew Murray or are just meeting him for the first time, these bite-sized reflections will lead you in a day-to-day development of a holy life.

Hard Cover ISBN 13: 978-0-936143-48-1

LIVING THE CHRIST LIFE

Compiled by Rebecca English

If you're serious about serving Christ, you've probably noticed how difficult it is to be genuinely holy and fruitful. *Living the Christ Life* combines gems from classic authors like Amy Carmichael, Andrew Murray and Vance Havner to create a practical daily devotional on living for Christ not in our strength, but in His.

ISBN 10: 0-87508-974-7
ISBN 13: 978-0-87508-974-4

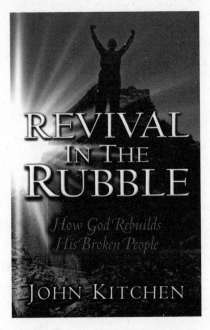

REVIVAL IN THE RUBBLE

John Kitchen

Rubble: the crumbled remains of a previous generation's true spiritual experience with God.

Can spiritual life and renewal ever be found in the midst of such devastation?

"Yes," says John Kitchen. "When God wants to do a fresh, reviving work in His people, He finds a person and breaks his heart."

"You'll be delighted with this user-friendly approach to allowing God to work in our hearts, bringing spiritual renewal out of brokenness."

— *Dr. Gary Benedict, President,*
Christian and Missionary Alliance

ISBN 13: 978-0-87508-873-0